ENDORSEMENTS

This book will make you homesick for your original home, Heaven! It will make you normal—that's normal according to the Bible!

SID ROTH
Host, *It's Supernatural!*

It has been said, "Every picture tells a story." Imagine 15 incredibly vivid visions of Heaven, revealing sights and wonders more glorious than you can imagine. *Encountering Heaven* takes us on a breathtaking journey, and seasons it with a clarion call to rethink how we live each day. Using her special gifts, Laurie has delivered more than just visions of Heaven; she has equipped us so we can daily encounter Heaven in even greater ways!

RABBI ERIC WALKER
Author/On-Air Host *Revealing the Truth*

After giving us bold challenges in *The Hell Conspiracy,* Laurie now graciously shares her testimonies about the revelations of Heaven in her new book, *Encountering Heaven.* Following the Apostle Paul's words *"I am not disobedient to the heavenly vision"* (Acts 26:10), she testifies about the goodness and the severity of God pointing us to the eternal love of Jesus Christ (Romans 11:22). Her enthusiastic testimonies are contagious!

DANIEL LIM
CEO, International House of Prayer Kansas City.

Once you get a taste of Heaven, it's impossible to view our time on earth the same. Laurie A. Ditto's encounters in *Encountering Heaven* will make you hungry to experience King Jesus as she does, and provoke the desire to tell everyone about the goodness of God. Grab a cup of coffee and enjoy tasting stories of Heaven!

ANA WERNER
Bestselling Author of *The Seer's Path*

Reawaken your mindset, emotions, and will to the eternity you were purchased for. Flame your desire, with practical truths from Encountering Heaven, to *"Go into all the world..."* (Matt: 28:18-20) and share the good news of our great God!

TRACY ECKERT
Executive Pastor of Storehouse Dallas
Author of *God's End-Time Temple*

The revelation experiences that Laurie A. Ditto has shared of Heaven and Hell are powerful and have made me more in awe of God. Through the pages of *Encountering Heaven,* be ready to glimpse revelations and understandings of what it means to see God's Kingdom come on Earth as it is in Heaven.

JOHN MATARAZZO
Host/Producer, AlongTheWay.Media

What's beyond the corridor of death no longer remains an obscure mystery. *Encountering Heaven* unveils the realm of angels, the reunion with loved ones, and the deeply intimate response of seeing Jesus. Each page renders secret insights of the invisible Kingdom to come. Time stands still as you are whisked beyond the veil revealing infinite mysteries and joys unspeakable!

WINSTON LOTT
Pastor, Blue Hills Church of the Nazarene

Laurie is a great storyteller, and her childlike enthusiasm makes this book deceptively profound. It is written with disarming simplicity and filled with scripture. I got lost in the beauty only to be confronted by my deep need for more of what Laurie understands about the Lord.

Encountering Heaven will deepen your love for Jesus, grow your vision of His Kingdom, and challenge you to share Heaven with everyone!

LUIS CATALDO

Intercessory Missionary, Vineyard Outreach America

Encountering Heaven takes us into the majestic beauty of the Kingdom of God and its angelic operations. Prepare to receive wisdom and revelation of eternity as you read the visions of these biblical realities and encounter the heart of Jesus!

DANIEL B. ALTMAN

Family Pastor, New Covenant Christian Church

I love supernatural testimonies of Heaven and Hell and God has taken Laurie A. Ditto to both places. These heavenly experiences have changed my life on earth and my relationship with God; I am more prepared for Heaven because of Laurie and her writings. Do yourself a great favor and read *Encountering Heaven* and God will talk to you!

HAL S. LINHARDT

Director, International Evangelists' Fellowship

If you're searching for answers about God and Heaven, this book *Encountering Heaven* will guide you and ignite your passion for Jesus and His Kingdom!

CHRIS FERGUSON

Senior Pastor, La Cygne Christian Church

Laurie's new book, *Encountering Heaven,* vulnerably traces her journey of encountering God in heavenly places. It delicately challenges any residue of performance mentality, while at the same time calls us higher in our interactions with Father God. We become more awake in understanding just how cherished we really are, and how our earthly interactions ultimately impact Him and eternity. Read, enjoy, and be inspired in your personal pursuit of God!

SHAWN BENSON

Senior Pastor, Harvest Fellowship Church

With a beautiful blend of narrative, personal testimony, and a captivating story line, Laurie A. Ditto has given us a very keen set of insights into the realities of Heaven. Find inside of *Encountering Heaven* a very refreshing and honest look at things that we have only dreamed of encountering someday. That someday is today!

MICHAEL KURLAND
Teacher, Hebrew Language

Laurie's stories and experiences are a reflection of her sincere faith in Jesus our Bridegroom and the "...*place he has prepared for those who love him*" (John 14:2-3). Be careful as you read—you will encounter Jesus yourself!

DALE ANDERSON
Sr. Pastor, *Calgary Full Gospel*, Canada

This book offers a tremendous amount of encouragement. It will alter mindsets to be about the Kingdom's business and reaching others with an eternal message of hope.

LARRY DUBLANKO,
Pastor, Cornerstone Church

ENCOUNTERING
HEAVEN

DESTINY IMAGE BOOKS BY LAURIE A. DITTO

The Hell Conspiracy

ENCOUNTERING
HEAVEN

---

15 SUPERNATURAL VISIONS OF HEAVEN
THAT WILL CHANGE YOUR LIFE FOREVER

LAURIE A. DITTO

DESTINY IMAGE® PUBLISHERS, INC.
P.O. Box 310, Shippensburg, PA 17257-0310
"Promoting Inspired Lives."

This book and all other Destiny Image and Destiny Image Fiction books are available at Christian bookstores and distributors worldwide.

Cover design by Eileen Rockwell
Interior design by Terry Clifton

For more information on foreign distributors, call 717-532-3040.
Reach us on the Internet: www.destinyimage.com.

ISBN 13 TP: 978-0-7684-5742-1
ISBN 13 eBook: 978-0-7684-5743-8
ISBN 13 HC: 978-0-7684-5745-2
ISBN 13 LP: 978-0-7684-5744-5

For Worldwide Distribution, Printed in the U.S.A.
1 2 3 4 5 6 7 8 / 25 24 23 22 21

DEDICATION

For Him, who is seated on the Throne.

"Immediately I was in the Spirit; and behold,

a throne was standing in heaven

and One sat on the throne."

—REVELATION 4:2 NASB

CONTENTS

CHAPTER 1

— ◆•◆ —

THE BRIDAL MARCH

*"For this reason we also, since the day we heard it,
do not cease to pray for you, and to ask that you
may be filled with the knowledge of His will in all
wisdom and spiritual understanding; **that you
may walk worthy of the Lord,** fully pleasing Him,
being fruitful in every good work and increasing
in the knowledge of God; strengthened with all
might, according to His glorious power, for all
patience and longsuffering with joy; giving thanks
to the Father who has qualified us to be partakers
of the inheritance of the saints in the light."*

—COLOSSIANS 1:9-12

The Kingdom of God is a real place! I know of many others who have experienced Heaven. People don't always share about it because it is often too difficult to put into words just how wonderful

Heaven is. All that to say, I'm not special because I've been there. Rather, it is the testimonies of what Heaven is like that help me endure whatever is necessary on earth to ensure that, in the end, I get to Heaven.

In this book, I will share about numerous visions, or visits as I lovingly refer to them. A vision is where your spirit is taken and shown something. They can happen while awake or sleeping. Oftentimes, I am given visions in part, and then after I research in the Bible what I saw I am given a continuation of that same vision. Without the study, I believe I would miss the importance of what God shows me in the visions.

Bringing those heaven ways and truths into our lives will change everything. I often try to share specific testimonies of Heaven to strengthen our faith.[1] For different reasons, Jesus has highlighted certain ones to share in this book. I believe that these were shown to me for the purpose of my continued salvation, and possibly for yours too. These realities are beyond my simple words, but my hope is that the few people being saved would be greatly multiplied!

Heaven operates in perfection! If we can understand why something works there, we can implement those principles here on earth.[2] I want all of those understandings to be alive inside of me so that the Kingdom of God is breaking out all around me and through me. I know that this is how I will do the things that Jesus did, and even greater things![3]

Many times, God sends angels to help as a guide. People ask if angels are assigned to everyone. I don't know if everybody has an angel, but I have one. If I will listen, my angel helps me when I am in trouble. I tend to believe that everyone has at least one. Let me share a couple of angel encounters to illustrate.

Once when I was leading an outreach in the inner city, my angel helped me out of a very dangerous situation. I had broken a couple of my own rules: know where you are at all times and do not go alone. To make a long story short, I was in a bad part of town and got turned around. A tough guy walked up to me and asked me why I was in his neighborhood.

I answered without hesitation. *"I am here for you, to tell you about Jesus!"*

I believe that my God sees and helps me especially when I am preaching the gospel. Whenever I feel afraid, I want to be sure that He is watching. Many times because of fear, I begin to worship or preach, whichever one is most appropriate. If the feeling of danger ramps up, I get louder!

This man did not look interested in hearing about Jesus. I felt danger approaching from around and behind me. More tough guys came and surrounded me. The situation did not look good for me.

I asked, *"How many of you guys have a relationship with the Savior, Jesus?"*

All of a sudden, the first guy looked behind me and asked, *"How many of those guys in white are with you?"*

I heard the voice of my angel telling me that he was near. I answered, *"All of them!"*[4]

The angel told me to turn around and walk toward his voice. I did just that. I never saw him or the ones he had brought with him to help me, but they were more than enough to cancel my desperate situation. It was as if my feet knew exactly where to go. My legs shook from the fear that was leaving my body. I started rebuking myself for being at the wrong place at the wrong time, but this was just more fear leaving my mind. I prayed and asked Holy Spirit to tell me what I should be thinking. I felt His pleasure and felt the word "brave" being increased as a reality in my spirit. Who knows? Maybe those men needed to encounter me just then. I am sure that my angel has helped me many times, especially when I couldn't physically do something.

Another time, I was on a roof trying to paint the front of some dormers for a friend. The house had three stories with the basement mostly exposed. The ladder and scaffolding were not high enough, so I climbed up on the shortest side of the roof and walked over to the tall side with the dormers. I painted one and was going over to the other one. I had not been paying attention to my energy levels. The calf of my leg began burning and cramping; I was forced to sit down. The slope of the roof was too steep for me in that state, and I began sliding off. I tried using my free hand to stop me, but to no avail. I began screaming for help, because I figured I was going to fall off the roof. Suddenly, I felt two hands slam against my chest and stop me.[5] I frantically tried to back up, but my calf spasm made it impossible. The hands that stopped me began steadily pushing me back and up to the peak.

I heard my angel, *"Be careful."*

I cannot tell you how grateful I am for that angel.[6] The importance of the task given to me by the Lord allows that angel to be assigned to me for that task, which boosts my confidence.

God gives visions for a profound purpose.[7] They are meant to direct, warn, change, terrify, and encourage.[8] This first vision should give us a glimpse of who we are as the Bride of Christ and walking out that reality in the here and now of our daily lives.

When I first arrived, I quickly realized that I was on my hands and knees. My back was hurting from the weight of what was on top of me. I could feel stress in my neck, tell that my shoulders were out, and I had a migraine headache. I was in total darkness and the overwhelming sense to quit life was running through my mind.

I could faintly hear the Lord asking, *"Where is she?"*

I couldn't tell where I was, but I knew I wouldn't be able to withstand the weight for much longer. All of my strength was being poured into these physical problems that I knew were caused by many consuming circumstances in my life. I could not answer Him because taking my focus off my problems was inconceivable.

I heard in the distance another very familiar voice answer Him. It was the voice of my angel. He had swooped under me and looked in my face. He appeared as a light. I knew that my eyes were open, but I was staring blankly in desperation.

I was glad that I was not alone and that my angel was at hand. With his help, I could win! I heard him answer the Lord. *"She's here under these circumstances."*

I'm thinking, *"Oh no!"*

All too often circumstances can cripple and capsize the best plans. I have taught on this subject before. However, teaching about it is not the same as going through it. God doesn't put us under circumstances; we do that to ourselves. Many times we need *help* from others to get free.

I heard the Lord say, *"Stand her up!"*[9]

My angel again appeared like a bright light, this time directly in front of my eyes. He said, *"Stand up!"*

I began to try, but it was the might of my angel that brought me up from the dark place where I could not see or live. He didn't need my might, just my agreement. The angels don't personally understand "choice." And although they do not force people they are assigned to help, they always obey the will of the Lord. I can't imagine the restraint they operate in or their confusion at our state of disobedience. After all, hell was created to accommodate those wicked angels, now demons, who chose rebellion.[10]

Now that I was standing, the new daylight and wide-open space was so refreshing. Instantly everything seemed better, and my problems appeared smaller. Sometimes just a new place can change everything. I looked up and I was in Heaven. The Lord, in His majesty and power, was standing at the top of the mountain and I was standing on a remarkable path. It was lined with fragrant flowers and had the purpose of bringing the Bride to the Bridegroom. I was in Heaven, and I was His bride. He was brilliantly magnificent and filled with light![11]

Just a second ago, I was willing to quit. I had no idea I was so close to seeing Him. I think that the hardest times are right before

He moves on our behalf. Waiting on God creates the ability to endure. His timing is a gift that strengthens us and should be treasured for what it produces.

Jesus smiled at me. The effect of His smile was life-giving! His pleasure over His creation is what makes a human heart come alive. I felt the effects from His smile on my physical body, and His pleasure was all I desired.

He called to me with excitement, *"Come!"*

I began walking. I was now on a bridal march. I looked down and noticed that I was wearing a stunning white wedding dress. However, I was dirty, and the dress had stains on it. Many of the stains came from the circumstances I was under. Others had been there for a long time. I needed a bath, and my dress needed to be cleaned. I was not happy that I was on the bridal march in that condition. Therefore, I was suddenly very self-conscious and wanted to stop.

My angel pointed for me to look up. Once I looked at Jesus again, I knew that He would make it all right and that everything was going to be OK. I could actually see my angel clearly. He was *big* and strong. He was striking with almost chiseled looks. He had on a brilliant white gown. I could see his wings, which meant he was on official business. He motioned for me to follow him on a different path, which looked like it would be more difficult than the other paths. He waited for me to pass him on the path. I looked around and saw other people who were also on their bridal march. Some people took the shortest route straight up the mountain. That way looked good to me too. My angel asked me to consider the long and difficult way.

What? Why would I want to go the long way? That made no sense to me. I wondered which way Jesus would recommend. My angel could somehow understand my dilemma. He smiled at me. I knew that he had been especially chosen for me—to help me achieve the purposes for which I was created.

I was reminded of a scripture that I struggle submitting to— where Jesus tells people to pick up their cross and follow Him.[12] My cross is not just a hard circumstance in my life, but rather it is obedience to the task the Lord has for me. I was glad my angel was there. He made it easier for me to obey. Ultimately, I had to trust that Jesus was going to be with me.

Trust is an unseen virtue that is powerful and living. Some-times the only way I can see something is through the trust that I have in the One who is guiding me into it. Jesus is my rear guard, and my angel is assigned to walk behind me. He was so big that he could see over and in front of me. Although it appeared that the direction I traveled was away from the Lord, I knew that the angel had heard His command so he could only help me achieve that goal. I walked down the path, and as I walked the terrain changed. It was not stable. It was a path less taken, and I was on a trailblazer-type adventure. There were different-looking people all around who were not wearing wedding clothes. Then, I realized it was because they didn't yet know Jesus and had no idea that the Lord has called His Bride to Himself.[13] These people were not on the same plain as the heavenly one where I could see Jesus on the mountaintop. I wondered how the vision of a heavenly walk could be mingled with the everyday affairs of the people on earth.[14]

The angel understood my confusion. He explained without words that I was in two places at the exact same time. My earthly body could only comprehend one reality at a time. That was why if I looked back, I would no longer see Jesus. He assured me the Lord was still watching me. Jesus was not restricted and could see in every reality with His resurrected body.

An understanding came to me that I should ask for gifts for these people.[15] This path, though less taken, would affect many others to become the Bride of Christ.[16] I was blessed to get to live this life on earth knowing that my bridal march would change many others. On it, I could ask Jesus for anything in His name in accordance with His will.[17] Through trust and faith in Him I could give my bridal gifts to them. Wow!

Nations go to war for their queen. This concept comes from the Lord and is a perfect picture of how Heaven is at war for the Bride of Christ. Think about the weddings you may have attended. Everyone watches for the bride. In fact, when she walks in, it is customary for everyone to stand at her entrance. For a short time, I was a wedding planner. Different parts of the wedding are more or less significant depending on the bride. However, the bridal march is always one of the most important.

Let me use our oldest daughter's wedding as an example. Due to a set of unique circumstances, her wedding was held in the mess hall of the local university. In a matter of hours, it was transformed into a beautiful venue. In fact, the administration was very excited to see the transformation. They took many pictures so that they could purchase similar items to make the room a wedding rental. Remarkably, the tiles on the floor had the exact colors of her wedding. The room had three tiers with the bottom level transformed into an altar. Mike and our daughter, Krystal, entered from an "exit" stairway at the very top of the room. She walked the long way around the whole level, passing all the guests who stood at beautifully decorated round tables. She paused before coming down onto the second level, looking down to where her groom, Andrew, stood. She repeated the process on the second level before stepping down onto the far side of the first level. The clapping for her wedding march was never ending. This march was much longer than a regular church aisle. She and Mike loved it! She was radiant. Mike was so proud of her and glad that he was able to show off his great love for our firstborn to our little world. Andrew waited expectantly at the bottom far end. He had eyes only for her.

My life on the earth is now my heavenly bridal march. I noticed that the first group of people I was approaching needed food. I prayed, thanking Jesus for His ever-watchful eyes upon me.[18] I told Him how grateful I am to be His bride and to have the privilege to invite everyone to join the march. I asked for His help, and for the authority to bless them, and that they may join in the celebration. With my love for Him increasing each time I shared about His identity, I grew in compassion, humility, and passion for the ones all around me.[19] Jesus granted me increasing authority in direct proportion to my growing love. People came to the saving knowledge of Jesus and began their own bridal march.[20]

With this bridal authority, whatever we ask from the Lord, He will give if the one asking believes in Him, His goodness, and His loving kindness.[21] Who on her wedding day would worry that the man she was marrying was not going to meet her basic needs? Or that she would have to beg him to assure her of his love?

As I left that first group, the path approached a fork. I could faintly see my angel who directed me to take the more difficult path. I caught a glimpse of my dress from the heavenly realm. It was becoming cleaner. Amazingly, beads and appliques were being added from each interaction on the journey.

The path was hard. No one had taken it in a long time. I was hot, tired, and hungry. I wasn't sure where I was, and I could feel danger all around me. I started feeling sorry for myself. Then the memory of being under those circumstances at the beginning of the vision reminded me that I am the Bride of Christ. I began humming "here comes the bride."

Suddenly, I was with a people in the mountains who needed a well. I wanted to help them and I knew to look up because the King was watching. I understood that even if I couldn't see Him, He would give me what I was asking for these people. It was my pleasure to jump in and help them, to tell them about my Bridegroom and His immense goodness. As the water began to spring forth, I laughed at His willingness to bless His bride on her walk.

Then people began surrounding me who were hurt, sick, and dying. I knew that I could help these ones too. My Jesus is the great Healer.[22] They just needed to know Him.

As I walked, the idea of the wedding of the King brought me much excitement. It would be the wedding of all time. And no one would want to miss it. I had an idea and began asking for the same gift over and over. I knew that each person whose eyes I met was important! So I asked the Lord that, if we met, I desired them as my gift to and for Him. And that their names would be written in the Book of Life so they could spend eternity with us.[23] I began asking and asking for the souls of people. I understood that they needed to exercise their choice, but my prayers were for those choices.

This vision changed me in many ways. I think of myself as His bride, so I act like it. I use my authority to bless others, especially in telling them about Him. I believe that His eyes are on me. I don't look for the shortcuts. The hard things don't cause me undue distress. I pay attention to the circumstances that can sabotage my march.

I make a point of stopping and looking into people's eyes. I cannot tell you how many times I have heard these things: *"You look very familiar."* Or, *"There's something about your eyes."* And, *"Do I know you?"*

God is living inside of me, and I want them to know Him.[24] In a wonderful way, I love them and their souls. I think that they remember the love of God from when He kissed them and started their lives on earth. I think that they can see Him and His love for them. How will they even know there is a wedding unless they are told, and how can they be told unless someone *goes* to tell them?[25]

There are no shortcuts to bridal authority in Christ.[26] It's one right decision and then another one. There are actions that create patterns and habits to help us do this. We are all on this march and we get to choose. There are shorter routes or longer ones that are hard and filled with many hard circumstances. It is important to remember that we can affect the homeless and hopeless. We can affect the teenagers who are confused and lonely. We can change neighborhoods, workplaces, and governments. We can affect our own families.

If we will take this bridal march seriously, we can ask for the gifts for others. We can dazzle the King with the beauty we create in our bridal gown by our acts of Christ's love.

May I suggest that you look for the long way? Make a portion of your march about the ones who need Christ. On this march, there is nothing the King won't give you. Think about that!

NOTES

1. Hebrews 11:34
2. Matthew 6:10
3. John 14:12
4. Psalm 34:7
5. Psalm 91:11
6. Daniel 3:28
7. Joel 2:28, Hosea 12:10
8. Hebrews 1:14, Psalm 91:11, Psalm 34:6-7, Matthew 18:10
9. Psalm 33:13
10. Matthew 25:41

11. 1 John 1:5
12. Luke 9:23, Matthew 16:24-26
13. Luke 15:10
14. Ephesians 2:6
15. 1 John 5:14-15
16. Jude 1:23
17. 1 John 5:4, John 14:13
18. Proverbs 15:3
19. Revelation 19:7
20. 1 Timothy 2:3-6
21. John 16:24
22. Exodus 15:26
23. Revelation 20:12
24. Ephesians 2:22
25. Romans 10:14-15
26. Romans 8:10

CHAPTER 2

MY GARDEN

"Thy will be done in earth, as it is in Heaven."

—MATTHEW 6:10 KJV

A lesson I have learned from visiting Heaven is that there is so much more of God's provision than what we access.[1] Jesus taught us to pray for the heavenly will of God to be a reality here on earth.[2]

In other words, we can have heavenly principles in our lives today. One reason for our lack of access to God's provision is that we don't know enough about how things work in Heaven. A second reason is that we don't know the Word of God well enough to apply His truths to our lives.[3] And third, we lack vision to see the personal changes needed to "live like Heaven."

I want to give you a little bit of backstory about this particular time I went to Heaven. I'm from upper Michigan, and ten of us ladies traveled in two cars to the International House of Prayer of Kansas City on a retreat. I was the group leader, and as such, I had one rule: no complaining.[4] This rule is important because when I start to complain, it is certain that everything goes downhill.

It was about a fourteen-hour trip to Kansas City. I had made the trip many previous weekends, and I never dreaded the drive because I love the International House of Prayer! During this trip, my husband, Mike, was on a missionary trip to Africa. Normally Mike helps me pack and prepare for our trips, but this time I did it on my own. I was much more stressed than normal because Mike wasn't around and I really wasn't confident in my ability to travel without him.

On the way down we had many problems. The check engine lights came on in both cars, we got caught in an ice storm, I was almost side-swiped by a semi-truck who didn't see me in the blind spot, and I discovered that the float in my car didn't work when I ran out of gas. We stopped over and over to deal with these issues and determine if we should keep going. I felt the strength from my spirit that we should keep going, but I was new to leaning into God, so I found myself stuck in the mental gymnastics of uncertainty. As the leader, I pressed on hoping my nervousness would somehow disappear, all the while presenting a confident front to the ladies.

As the miles wore on, frustrations mounted inside each car and the ladies started arguing with one another. If we had started out in unity, we had certainly lost it along the way. The normal four-teen-hour trip had taken twenty long and stressful hours. I just wanted to go to bed. It started as the worst trip ever.

Upon arrival, we checked into our housing and found that we needed to visit the grocery store. The ladies needed to de-stress and I needed some time alone, so I offered to handle the shopping for our necessities. The frustrations of our trip continued when I found that the recommended grocery store was closed by the time I arrived. I headed to a local gas station and received directions to another store. The directions were complicated and aggravated me further. To make matters worse, the store didn't have many of the items we needed. To make matters even worse, the directions back to our housing were impossible. I got very lost.

When I finally returned, I was met with a roaring argument. Instead of de-stressing, they had ramped things up. Being the leader, they looked to me. Unfortunately, I had no patience and yelled at everyone to stop being so petty. I unloaded all of my frus-trations and everything that the group had done to bother me and sent them all to bed! This was definitely not the best way to begin a retreat. I had broken my own rule of not complaining. And now I was reaping the devastating results.

I didn't sleep well that night. One of the ladies was crying. Another let me know that she wished she had not come. I was filled with so much negativity. I wanted to do exactly what these ladies were doing, but as the leader I couldn't show them. Instead, I hid and cried in the shower realizing I had behaved exactly as they had.

The next morning, I got up extra early to walk over to the International House of Prayer. I was still upset, cranky, and now hungry. I wished that someone else were the leader. I was embarrassed by my actions the night before. My plan was to "hide" in the Prayer Room. Maybe God could download a plan to fix everything.

I tell you all of this backstory because people ask what I was doing when Jesus took me to Heaven. I believe that God can take anyone to Heaven at any time regardless of the state of our body, mind, will, or emotions.[5] The Bible says, "Blessed is he who is pure in heart, for you shall see God."[6] This came to my mind, and I started praying it.

"God, make me pure in heart, because I want to see You. I need to see You!" I pray this often when I am in a really negative mood. It helps me plumb line to the reality of how off-course I am and how to get back into alignment.

Some of the ladies from our group came into the prayer room. They were still upset and wanted to tell me about it. I had no idea how to help them so I recommended that we each pray for an hour and then gather the whole group to talk.

I was stressed. Didn't they know that I had my own problems? I needed to disappear. I wasn't sure where to hide until I had a great idea. I went to the very front row and laid down across the chairs. This way, unless someone walked up to the front row they wouldn't know I was there. But God knew *exactly* where I was.

I lay down with my knees and my face toward the back of the chairs, and I began complaining to God. You know you can complain to God, and it's called prayer, right? So I was dumping all kinds of stuff on Him. Stuff from the ladies, the cars, from home, from my fear of Mike being gone, and a hundred other worries. I was complaining to Him about everything including my own inadequacies.

"I don't know how to fix all these problems, God!" is probably my most common prayer. I am sure I must have used it then too. I started crying for myself, feeling sad and full of self-pity. I wanted to be a good leader, good mom, and good wife. A leader should know what to do, and I certainly didn't. I couldn't fix anything—not for me, my children, my family, or this group. I really worked myself up into a crying fit. When I am in one of those pity parties, I can go really low, quickly. Then, suddenly, my mind went to sleep. While my mind was sleeping, God began talking to me, telling me things.

I thought, *"Wow, I would have never thought of that!"* And more answers came to me. *"I would never have believed You could do that, Jesus."* And I recall thinking, *"I'm never going to forget this."* But somehow I can't remember now what the Lord told me during that time. Although I cannot remember His words, I know that He spoke them to my spirit, and they are mine to keep. My spirit is the keeper of His truths, so they are safer than if I could remember them.[7] At that point, I was no longer complaining, but I was in a nice mental place.

In an instant, I was in Heaven, and I was there because Jesus wanted to help me. I thought He was going to give me answers for the ladies, a plan to get us back on track. I couldn't have been more wrong. The Bible says that His ways are not our ways, which is true, but I believe that they can be.[8]

Suddenly I was in the most beautiful park-like garden imaginable. It was huge and went on for as far as I could see. Two angels were escorting me to the Lord. The grass under my feet was perfect, so thick that not one more blade could fit. As I stepped on it, the grass pushed me upward, helping me walk, because it was alive and had supernatural strength. It was so beautiful and rolling. It didn't roll because the land was sloped, but because the grass wanted to roll. Incredible!

Around me there were many people enjoying the grass, because it massaged our feet with its movement. The people of Heaven were amazing and perfect! They only thought good things, they were filled with hope, they enjoyed *everything*, and they were excessively joyful.[9] Each person dressed in the clothes from their time period. So seeing one woman with a bustled dress laughing with one in a toga was "normal." There were men in kilts talking to others wearing long robes. But each person was perfect! I loved looking at the beautiful heavenly people. They made my eyes happy to watch. The most impressive thing to look at were the eyes of the heavenly people. It was much like when you look into the sparkle in the eyes of a baby and how it brings you peace. We see Jesus in the innocence in that child's eyes. In Heaven, we get lost looking into each other's eyes, which are alive in God.

Not only did the huge park have stunning grass and exceptional people, there were amazing trees, beautiful flowers, water fountains, pools, and statues. I saw gates into special garden areas and walkways that meandered through lovely sitting areas. The most amazing flowers and shrubs surrounded the garden, filled with a beauty as stunning as the heavenly people and intoxicating fragrances.

The garden was filled with a peaceful "soul hum." Our souls, when they are this kind of happy, make noise, kind of a "do-a-little-ditty." Each soul was humming along with everyone else's in an incredible harmony that created the most wonderful atmosphere! Amazingly, we could hear each other's souls, and together we made a melodious soul hum. This is the background noise in Heaven.

The garden was filled with beautifully shaped trees with leaves of every color like I have never seen on earth. The trees expressed all the seasons at once. On each one, I saw the flowers, the fruits, and the different colored leaves. These remarkable trees grew in unique ways that showed their astounding beauty. They mesmerized me. Their trunks even did things that are impossible here on earth, such as creating a swing inside itself. In addition, the trees joined in with the melodious soul humming.

But the absolutely most remarkable things in the garden were the statues. In each area there was a memorial set up in the form of a statue. Of course, Jesus was a part of each statue, and His being *with* the people made them important. There were statues of Him with an apostle, with a martyr, or playing with children. It was so impressive and made me wonder who all of them were and what the full story was behind each statue.

They were not like statues on earth. Instead they were the Lord's living memory. They were in vivid color and emitted the emotion that Jesus felt about the statue. My words cannot do justice to the beauty and awe of His memory statues. Even "memory" isn't quite the right word because time for the Lord is not like ours with past, present, and future.

Each trip to Heaven allows me to notice something more about Heaven. Most times I don't understand the concept or lesson of the trip until I come back. The thing I always notice is how much I like myself when I am in Heaven. When we are in Heaven, we don't have negative thoughts about ourselves or anyone else.[10] Those thoughts aren't allowed there, and so we shouldn't have them here. We really love ourselves in Heaven!

After noticing all of these wonderful details, I suddenly could see the Lord in the distance. He was down a hill of rolling grass surrounded by a large crowd of heavenly people. I noticed the combined dazzling brilliance of the color of their clothes. Individually, they each wore a certain color, but joined in the group, the color of the clothes was very unique. It was a compilation of every single color on earth and colors only found in Heaven, all compressed together. They were bright, vibrant, alive colors that moved and changed. Imagine taking all these colors and putting them into a small compressed dot, something like a sequin. Amazingly, somehow all these colors worked together and created white light, a brilliant light that magnified when joined to the Lord. So even though the clothes were different styles, they all created this most stunning and breathtaking reflection in honor of the Lord.

As the heavenly people came into the presence of Jesus, all their clothes began working together in union to express something different. His brilliance caused the clothes to change so that they became a beautiful, white sparkling light.[11] But it was so much more.

I was seeing everything working together perfectly. People are stunningly brilliant, reflecting the presence of the Lord. Even now, I cry at remembering. Only Jesus is the superstar. Everyone knows it, yet He causes His people to shine.

Although Jesus was surrounded by so many important people and angels, He stood out as He *always* does. His clothes were different than everyone else's—clothes that only He wears. It was like there was a time period of clothes that were specifically made for the King in the time before time. Of course, His clothes were a cut above, not because of a certain tailor, but because of the absolute perfection radiating inside the God-Man, Christ. Because of this, Jesus' clothes shone, and I saw that there was no comparison to His authority, superiority, or holiness.

Something else that I learned in Heaven is how angels dress. When angels wear their wings, they are in what would be their military uniform or on assignment, but they don't always wear their wings. When they are on certain assignments, they show their military uniform (wings), but when they're doing other assignments their wings don't show. The angels escorting me had their wings and so did the ones with Jesus. I knew that whatever they were telling Him, it was serious. As the angels moved closer to Him, the people around Him began to move quietly away.

The whole picture changed and appeared very serious. Jesus asked them a question, *"Where is she?"*

I could hear in Heaven everything that was said about me. Nothing about me was hidden from me. Sometimes the Lord lets this happen here on the earth. I can "hear" things about me, and then I don't struggle with my own understanding. Isn't it amazing that in Heaven, no one talks about you behind your back? Instead, people talk about you for you to *know*.

I realized, *"He's looking for me."*

At first it made me really happy to know He was looking for me. But as He asked, the angels escorting me moved me in an instant to be with Jesus. To know that God wanted to talk to me made me feel pretty special, but at the same time it felt very unnerving.

Has there ever been a time that you couldn't talk to a loved one and you couldn't reach them when you needed to tell them something important? And then you finally get to talk to them, and there is a huge relief that comes from knowing that all is right. I felt that with Jesus. I felt a heart connect with Him because He is so willing to show us the depths of His heart and let us keep what He has there as the unchanging truth. So before I reached Jesus, I had all these questions, worries, and anxieties.[12] But as soon as I stood before Him, it all dropped away. What I wanted to say or ask didn't matter any longer. It only mattered what He wanted to say. Just breathing in His presence took all the worries away. Gone forever.

He was waiting for *me*. Unthinkable! The angels with the Lord turned and looked up the hill in my direction and pointed toward their fellow angels. I was excited until I looked down.

You would not believe what I was wearing! Suddenly I realized that I was not reflecting the beauty of the King. I was not wearing the beautiful white clothes like everyone else. I was not in a beautiful time period outfit. I was in the trashiest red dress you have ever seen. They don't dress like that in Heaven. In Heaven all the clothes are modest. This trashy dress was cut way too low in the front, extremely immodest. It was three or four sizes too small. I knew that the V on the backless dress showed part of my bum. There was no way to cover up. I wanted to disappear.

I thought, *"This can't be! I don't want to meet the Lord like this!"*

The angels motioned for me to come closer, but I didn't move on my own, so the angels nearby moved me. In Heaven you do not disobey. I could tell they were not impressed with me.

Now I was beside the Lord, and I panicked. I was trying not to stand up in front of Him, and yet because that is what He wanted, I did His will. He looked in my eyes, and He was so excited to see me. His eyes were very beautiful and very welcoming. Joy danced in them like flames of fire.[13] His hands, with the marks on His wrists very noticeable, reached for my face.[14] It was one of the deepest emotional ways that God has touched me, because touching someone's face is an intimate gesture of love. As He touched my face, I started backing up.

"No! No! No, Lord! Don't touch me! I'm unclean!"[15]

The joyful fire in His eyes changed. The Lord was serious. I was shocked. He was unnerved. When I talked to God in Heaven, I just cut to the chase. There was no small talk or putting up fences to ensure that I was understood. Jesus already understood

25

everything better than I did anyway. I've applied this lesson when I speak with Him now. I just cut to the chase and tell Him what's wrong, because He already knows.

He asked, *"What are the charges?"*

His question pulled an answer out of me and my words began spilling out of my heart to Him. Tears were streaming down my face.

I answered: *"I don't believe that I am who You say I am. I don't believe I'm going to do what You said I'm going to do. I can't be a leader! I am a nobody. I will never get it right."*

He said: *"Continue."*

The depths of the poisoned, stinking thinking in my own self surprised me. Somehow deep, unknown layers tied to other parts of me held on to pain that I did not know about. Jesus waited, knowing there was more. Answers continued pouring from my heart.

"I don't believe You, Jesus!"

Here I was, standing in front of God Almighty who had never done anything to ever let me down, but still I told Him.

He said, *"Continue."*

"I don't think I'm smart. I don't think I'm beautiful. I don't think I'm made the right way." And the list went on and on. It was as if every time He said, *"Continue,"* He forced all the crud out of me.

"I don't believe You're going to do what You said You are going to do. I don't believe that You really love me. I don't believe You have all control on earth. I don't believe You answer prayers for people like me. I don't believe that I am your favorite."

Then, out of nowhere, I said to Him, *"Lord, I am a prostitute!"*

I was shocked by the prostitute part. I've sinned a lot on the earth, but I haven't sinned in that way. However, as soon as I said it, I knew that I had sinned in that way. My spirit told the truth to a holy God. Prostitutes will use themselves to get what they want. I have used the gifts of God to try to manipulate Him and others. I could see that I was a prostitute.

Please understand that these things do not belong in Heaven. However, instead of casting me out because of that stinking thinking, He pulled those thoughts out of me to get rid of them. It was like throwing up all over the place. I couldn't stop it, and Jesus was not going to stop until it was all out.

Finally, He declared the truth over me, *"You are mine!"*

I looked at Him and He was smiling. He said *"Laurie."*

When the Lord said my name, I felt so good, so right. He said it with so much love and appreciation. He said my name in such a way that I wanted to hear Him say it all the time.

He said, *"Laurie, all those things were true before you met Me."*

I just needed God's stamp of approval on my life. As soon as I understood that I am a new creation in Christ, in a new bloodline—the bloodline of Christ that enabled me to take my thoughts captive.[16] But I had to do my part and agree with one thing: I am His.[17]

Because He said that I am His, I understood it could not be undone. It was finished. As He spoke that over me, everything changed. He bound up those terrible things about me by His confession of ownership over me.

I looked at my dress again.

He said, *"Laurie, nobody can see your clothes except you."*

Everyone around us only saw what He saw. He had hidden me and all of that yuck, all of that exposure, and all of the "I don't believe You." The scriptures say that love covers a multitude of sins, and He covered me while I was there.[18] He so wonderfully wrapped me in His love that no one could see anything else. His brilliance was so bright that all anyone could see was Him. As I looked again at my dress, it changed into what they all saw. It became the most beautiful gown made out of that beautiful material I had seen on the others in Heaven. I knew that He had chosen this perfect dress for me. Not only was it beautiful, but it radiated my beauty. Beside Him, it radiated *His* beauty. I was perfect.

Then He stuck His arm out. This gesture meant that He, Himself, was going to escort me. The angels stayed back as we walked away. He offered His right arm like a gentleman would escort a lady. I placed my left arm out on top of His.

Then He said, *"Come with Me."*

We began walking. The Lord loves to walk with us. He walked me around in the gardens until we were in what was my favorite place. I felt it. This part of the park-like garden was one of the most special parts, although I didn't yet understand. It was as if it was made just for me. The garden was filled with all kinds of flowers that I knew and loved and many I had never seen before. There were beautiful benches with soft cushions. The Lord kept walking with me while enjoying my excitement as I encountered the different areas.

As we walked, I paid no attention to where I was, because being with Him was where I longed to be. He was headed to a particular stop. We sat down on a swing-type bench. I love to swing, and this bench was just the right height for my legs. I looked up and noticed a statue. It was a beautiful statue surrounded by flowers. It was of Jesus as He was dancing with a woman whom He loved. The first thing I noticed was that she was wearing a dress like I was wearing. The dress He had just given me. No, wait, it was me! I knew that the statue was of me. I was so excited to be there! God had made this special spot of the beautiful garden for me.

He looked at me and said, *"Thank you."*

Isn't it amazing that He would say thank you because I let Him help me? Without His help, I would be nothing! Without His covering, I would have been exposed. Tears filled my eyes as I shook my head. I should be the one to say thank you. Here on display was His living memory of me.

There's always fire in the Lord's eyes.[19] Always. There's a fire of love, a fire of fighting for something, a fire of when He's trying to make a wrong thing right.[20] But when I looked into His eyes, I knew what I wanted to do. However, before I could do anything, I had to *be* His. I had to know that I am beautiful, fun, smart, kind, a worker bee, and the "good" list went on and on. I believed in Jesus! I believed that He would accomplish everything that He set out to do. I believed that I was important and that I needed to run to Him instead of away from Him.

He smiled at me, and I felt Him tell me to remember. I knew it would be hard, but not impossible. I knew that to live like I was still in Heaven while back on earth, I must be completely His as I had been in Heaven.

I reacted in the most intimate way He had taught me. I reached my hand up to touch His life-giving face. I could tell by His eyes that this was right. Before my hand fully touched Him, I was back on earth.

It was so beautiful. As I was leaving, He said, *"Thank you."* His voice filled me up. Who are we that God should say thank you to any of us? But when God said thank you to me, I knew I had done something that pleased Him.[21]

What was it that pleased God? I have thought about it long and hard so that I can repeat it. God was pleased by me giving Him "the yuck" in my life. When I had submitted who I thought I was to Him, I had agreed with the truth that I am *His*.

Now, I don't doubt that He loves me. I saw the wounds on Him. No one should ever, ever doubt Him. There is no King, no God, who has ever done what our God has done for us. He loves us! We are dressed in the righteous deeds that He sets up for us, and sometimes those righteous deeds are just to believe in who God is and what He declares.[22] Then, once He perfects it in us, He creates a memory statue. Something unchanging to help us know He wants us to remain that way—His finished work.

Jesus has gone ahead of us to prepare a way, a room, a garden, and a statue.[23] Believe! Whenever yuck seems to find its way into us, we don't have to wait until we get to Heaven to get rid of it. We need to get on our knees and confess: *"God, this is what I'm struggling with. I'm struggling with a promise. I thought it would have been answered by now. I'm having a hard time waiting."*

As we tell Him, He changes our garments from trashy ones into perfectly fitting ones that reflect His light.[24] Then we can take a walk with Him. Take some time. Dial down. It's His mighty right hand that He extends. He lets us put our left hand onto His powerful right hand that He will use to fix the wrong things.

When I came back, I realized how happy I was in Heaven. Happiness there grows on itself like a crystal. The beauty goes to the core. I think if the people of Heaven lived on earth, they would aggravate us because they are so happy. They just become more and more happy. Their eyes are happy. They laugh. They have fun. There's no sickness, no disease. There are no problems. God has made a place that is beyond anything that we can think or imagine. Heaven is wonderful!

It's waiting for us. Any hard thing that we have to go through will be worth it if we can keep our hearts and our thoughts and our actions from falling into a yucky place.[25] The Bible already says our hard times are just a momentary light affliction.[26]

Now that I was back in the Prayer Room, I knew that I could handle helping the team. One of the ladies came to tell me that a prophecy team was waiting for us all. They had approached her to explain that they had an opening.

Once inside the room, the prophecy leaders excitedly told us how God had them praying for a group from *Michigan*. They felt especially compelled to pray for the leader. They asked who the leader was, and everyone pointed to me. They told me that Jesus has a special encounter waiting for me that would build my faith in Him and be mine forever. *Wow!* They also told me that I would know because He would say the words "Thank you."

Each of us needs to know that God has a place waiting for us. It's not just any place, but one where He has memorialized the times when we were stuck in a struggle and let Him help us out of it. It is important to understand that once we overcome our struggles, they leave beautiful markings in us and in Heaven. And because of this principle, we can *live like we live in Heaven.* We need to help others using songs, scriptures, testimonies, and His compassionate eyes of fire.[27] It is going to be great when we get there. But Jesus wants it to be great for us now.[28] When I feel someone needs help, I do what He taught me. I place my hands on their face, look deep into their eyes, and tell them who they are. They might not know it, but my actions can remind them to live like they are in Heaven.[29]

NOTES

1.   1 Corinthians 2:9

2.   Matthew 6:10

3.   2 Timothy 2:15

4.   Philippians 2:14-16

5.   Psalm 115:3

6.   Matthew 5:8

7.   Proverbs 3:5-6

8.   Isaiah 55:8-9

9.   Revelation 21:4

10. Revelation 21:27

11. Psalm 104:2

12. 1 Peter 5:7

13. Revelation 19:12

14. John 20:24-29

15. Isaiah 6:5

16. 2 Corinthians 10:5

17. Song of Solomon 2:16

18. 1 Peter 4:8, Proverbs 10:12

19. Revelation 19:12

20. Revelation 1:14, Song of Solomon 8:6

21. Hebrews 11:5, Ephesians 5:10

22. Revelation 19:8

23. John 14:2

24. Revelation 7:9

25. Romans 8:18

26. 2 Corinthians 4:17

27. Ephesians 5:19-20

28. Hebrews 10:24-25

29. 1 Timothy 4:12

CHAPTER 3

---◆▪◆---

AMUSEMENT PARK

*"Trust in the Lord with all your heart, and
lean not on your own understanding."*

—PROVERBS 3:5

Everyone needs to know about Heaven! It helps us not give up and is especially important for those who are sick in their bodies or in their hearts. As times get hard, we need to know about our eternal resting place so that we don't quit. Children need to know about Heaven so that when they grow up, they stay away from the perversion and seduction of sin.[1] Sharing about Heaven is a great way to help people realize the many truths about Jesus Christ.

On another trip to Heaven, I arrived in Heaven's amusement park, which was much bigger than Disney World. The day was a special day on Heaven's calendar. It was a day set aside for the children. There are a lot of children who live in Heaven, including many babies who never took a breath on the earth, but in Heaven they are alive and extremely joyful.[2] In fact, they were some of the most amazing people I met in Heaven! I will call them "practically perfect people."

In times past, it was considered an honor to have a priest in the family, but in Heaven it is an honor to have a practically perfect person in your line. Although I have called them "practically perfect people," I cannot give you their actual title because it is not a title but rather a heartfelt brightness that they achieve. They are the ones who were never actually born into sin. They were invited by God to come to Him before they were born. These are the babies we call miscarried, but the plan for them was not miscarried at all. These children were wanted by their earthly parents and created in love. Then suddenly they took their place as "practically perfect people." They are the closest people, in their brightness, to the Lord. These children know they are deeply loved and that their parents will be with them soon. (Since this vision to Heaven, I have a grandbaby who is now a "practically perfect person." I know beyond a doubt that he/she is wonderfully cared for and in a very short time, we will all be together.)[3]

In Heaven, there are also intentionally aborted babies who are also very bright like God. He has brought them to Himself. He covers these ones in a very special way too. Again, it is not a title but a heart brightness that distinguishes them. For explanation, I will call them, "His happy hearts."

For the parents who deeply regret the decision they made to abort, they will shed tears of joy when they meet their children, if they make it to Heaven. And there are parents who ached to have children on the earth and could not, for one reason or another. The babies without parents in Heaven will be theirs.

All of these "practically perfect people" and "His happy hearts" are waiting for their parents according to the promise the Lord has given to them.

If you do not currently love children, I want to invite you to get to know some because there is a piece of the human heart that comes alive by loving children. In Heaven, our hearts love everyone but especially children who model "childlikeness" with such perfection. This is true in our everyday life as well. We can make our lives so much better by learning to love children.[4]

On the day I arrived, everyone was going to the amusement park in honor of the childlikeness gift that God had created for us all. Grownups were the workforce at the amusement park, unless a parent was with their child. Of course, then they went on the rides with the children. God loves to have fun, and He wants people to have fun too! The work in Heaven is always enjoyable, but the "play work" was especially enjoyable. It is said that God has a reputation of being "the best ride-riderer, ever!"

I arrived early. The park was not open yet as the day was still new. This made me happy, as I naturally do not like to be late. I was assigned by an angel to work with the man who was working at the kiddie coaster. This was the beginners' roller coaster. The man was an exceptionally happy older gentleman. As the angel brought me to him, the angel bowed. The man gave the angel a hug and thanked him for bringing me right over.

As the angel left, I noticed how very bright the man was. The angel had grown brighter being near the man. My conclusion was that when heavenly people get together, they get collectively brighter. Now in Heaven my brain worked differently. I knew a lot more stuff there than I knew on earth. Also, in Heaven I am related to everybody. It was the biggest family reunion, and it was awesome! I knew everybody, and once introduced I didn't forget anyone's name. In Heaven, we communicated heart to heart, so no one is ever misunderstood. No one has to go back and try to explain what they meant and go through, *"When you said that, it made me feel this way."* Misunderstandings don't happen there because our hearts speak and the other person's heart receives. So the communication is heart to heart more than it is voice to voice.

I figured that I was there to work with this wonderful older gentleman. At first, I thought he might need my help. *Hah!* I was so wrong!

He was excited to be with me and to show me the ropes on the little roller coaster. It was small enough to barely be considered a roller coaster. I remembered a time when my daughter was very young and we took her to the carnival. There was a little roller coaster that really scared her. I had to stop the ride to help her off. The kind man knew my thoughts, and I felt his pleasure over my memory of getting her off the ride.

One of the things that I "knew" in Heaven was that this man *always* chose this first ride. And he made sure that "fear" never entered the heart of a child. Just as satan's disobedience had no place in Heaven, neither does fear. The gentleman was so patient, kind, and gentle.[5] More like *patient, kind,* and *gentle!* He made sure every little one knew that he or she was safe and, in so doing, he taught them how to trust. Even though the rides didn't have safety straps, there was never going to be an accident in Heaven. As he explained to me, it is not the strap that defeats fear, but it is trust.[6]

I was impressed that the first ride would help children to learn to trust. He explained that as he placed the child into the seat, he assured them of his love for them. He told them what to expect and let them know the purpose of the roller coaster was not only to have fun, but also to learn to trust every ride in the park. He explained that everyone has to pass this ride to enter the park. Then they could join adventures outside the park. Even I would have to pass this ride of faith to enter.

The training continued while we checked each little seat on the roller coaster. He shared that trust is built by someone important who keeps their word; by someone being patient, kind, and understanding. He asked me about my understanding of those words.

He was so easy to talk to, and I explained that on the earth we struggle with trust. His eyes tried to meet mine, but I looked away. I continued with how, in fact, I struggle with patience, kindness, and being understood by others. I admitted that I have a hard time trusting. He asked me whom I trust. I asked if I could get back to him on that answer. He laughed, letting me off the hook.[7]

He explained that children in Heaven don't struggle with trust because trust is built over time with layers of certainty in everyone they meet.[8] It is a foundation stone in Heaven that comes alive in all the people. *Wow!* I had no idea how that might happen. He said that this was how it was originally designed to work on earth too, but it had been broken.

This gentleman was so excited to be talking with me. Because we were there extra early, we had time to sit and talk. He told me about amazing adventures he had experienced. I was all ears. He shared about chasing stars and riding a whale. He told about hiding treasures in deep caves for others to find and touching the bottom of the ocean. Each adventure was remarkable. He was an amazing storyteller, and with each story I too desired to try the same things. He shared how one generation serving the next is the Designed Order. That through the generations, trust is grown.

He shared how in Heaven, we can still serve. As the adults began coming to work the different stations in the amusement park, I was wondering, *"Where should I fit in?"*

The gentleman heard my thoughts and asked, *"Would you like to fit in?"*

I knew that he could do any of the jobs from the cotton candy to the submarine ride. I knew he would be willing to do every job. Instead of answering his question, I asked him why he didn't choose a different ride. He told me that it was because at the first ride you are given wisdom that lets you know that "you fit in." I smiled at him, I wanted to fit right here, right now.

I really liked the man. I liked his wide smile and his gentle hands that seemed as large as bear paws. I showed him how I could bend my fingers back, just like a child would show off. He laughed and told me how beautiful my hands were. As he said it, I believed. I asked him if I could tell him something that was probably a lie, but that I had a hard time fighting. He then told me, *"You have always been afraid that you don't fit in."*

How did he know?

It felt so freeing to know that he knew already and I didn't have to stumble trying to not look needy. I looked into his beautiful eyes, and suddenly I could feel in my heart that I fit with him and that I would *always* fit with him. Because he was never going anywhere, because Heaven is eternal, my relationship with him would be *forever*. I was almost overcome with emotion.

When I get nervous, I switch the conversation. I do it very skillfully, usually. I knew he knew I was working hard to maintain my composure, and he let me. I asked about the children coming. He was very excited about everyone who was coming. He knew all their names. He could tell me about each one and how special they are to him.

I asked, *"How do you deal with pushiness?"*

He answered, *"There's no pushing and no shoving in Heaven. Children with that personality that just can't wait are allowed to go to the front of the line, and nobody gets upset because there's plenty of time."*

Then I asked, *"Is time used to help them become patient? Why are they not instantly patient?"*

He gave a wonderful belly laugh and said, *"Childlike impatience is not bad like disobedience; instead, it is a wonderful gift called excitement. Excitement is a staple of Heaven."*

He went on to share how excited he is when the little ones can't wait to come hug him. Because time is never an issue, he has time to listen to them, and he feeds them wonderful foods that I had never seen before.

To try to understand, think of cotton candy and how it is such an enjoyable treat at a carnival. In Heaven there is some type of fruit that is sweet like cotton candy but so much better. No matter how hard someone tries, there is no way to drink all the juice, it just runs everywhere. Everybody laughs watching each other try to eat this fruit and not make a mess. The great joy it brings is not easily explained.

I watched as others ate the fruit. I laughed as they tried. He invited me to try one. Oh my goodness! He told me that no one could eat it and drink the juice in a dripless manner. I loved the challenge, and so I tried. Immediately, at the first tiny bite, I began laughing. This fruit knew it was the game, and it had never lost. It exploded juice at me. The gentleman laughed his belly laugh, and I laughed harder. Everyone was laughing. It was wonderful![9]

I asked him if he ever goes on some of the other rides with the children. He said yes. He loves to ride them all. And he goes with anyone who asks. He could tell I was confused because I knew he would never leave the baby roller coaster ride.

He explained that this first ride was for beginners, the ones who couldn't trust. People only rode it once, and then they went on to the big rides like the Ferris wheel. (I cringed at the thought of the Ferris wheel.) He explained that outside of the park is where children choose to do amazing adventures with God. But to do those exploits, the child must be fearless. The park was designed to keep children childlike and train them to trust God. It was all done in fun because fun isn't fearful, just exciting. Every new child has an appointment with this ride. He is actually the man who makes the appointment; then the angel brings the person right to him.

He began telling me about the Ferris wheel and why it had so scared me before. I was shocked that he knew why I was afraid of the Ferris wheel. He explained that the ride here let everyone see the whole park, and at the top you could find your location in respect to another ride. He said that many times this ride helped children figure out where they had been and where they wanted to go. It was a ride on which to rest. He recommended that children ride it several times to be sure of their surroundings and directions. As he spoke about the gifts built inside the experience of the Ferris wheel, I decided I wanted to go on it, but only with him.

I was very quiet. After a time of silence, he reached for my hand and said, *"You don't have because you don't ask."*[10]

It was as if a box of unanswered questions had been opened inside of me and suddenly I needed the answers. Some questions were about me, some about tomorrow, and then the most important question came quickly to the forefront of my mind.

"Who am I to you?"

He answered, *"I am your Father, and you are My child. You will need My trust inside you so that you can trust Me."*[11]

Somehow, the Father, that gentle operator, had taken me on the beginner's roller coaster ride. The angel reappeared and bowed.

I bowed, too. The Father reached out and hugged us both. The angel had a list of God-sized adventures with my name on them. I was excited to get started. I asked if I could ride the Ferris wheel before I left. Father was very pleased and told me that He would always join me when I reached the very top. I believed Him, because I trusted Him.

God made me a person who loves to be on adventures with Him. It is wonderful to enjoy a ride when things in life are easy. But it takes special remembrance to not grow fearful when things in life are difficult. When I get frazzled in day-to-day life, I often will find a quiet place and close my eyes so that I can picture myself on the first ride again. In this quiet place, I can hear Him ask me the very questions I need to highlight the problem. Of course, He always knows the problem, and in His kindness He helps me see it too. Once I understand, I can give the problem to Him and trust that He is with me on this difficult ride. Each time we finish a day's adventures, my trust grows because He is trustworthy.

NOTES

1. Proverbs 2:6
2. Matthew 19:14
3. Matthew 18:1-3
4. Matthew 19:14
5. Philippians 4:5
6. Proverbs 3:5-6
7. Exodus 34:6, Psalm 145:8
8. Psalm 56:3

9. Psalm 126:2

10. James 4:2-3

11. 2 Corinthians 6:18, 1 John 3:1

CHAPTER 4

---◆◆◆---

HEAVENLY TRUTHS

"The Lord says, 'My thoughts are not like your thoughts. Your ways are not like my ways.'"

—ISAIAH 55:8 NCV

L ife in Heaven is very different than on earth. Heaven is a King-dom.[1] Jesus, the God/Man rules it. We may think we understand this, but I challenge whether we really grasp this truth. I have not spe-cifically shared the following heavenly truths in the other chapters, but understanding these truths will afford a better framework for the visions here. Now is a good time to ask God for His help in giving us living understanding. The Word of God is living and current, and by the power of the Holy Spirit, He can bring understanding that is life-giving.[2]

ACCESS

The Kingdom of God is founded in holiness.[3] This holiness of Heaven cannot and will not be polluted. Sin and holiness are incompatible and can never be together. Think of two strong magnets that are repelling each other. The only way they can come together is if they are polarized the correct way.

In Heaven everything reflects God, much like a mirror image. He created everything, so each thing is able to reflect the part of God that is unique to them. Or let me say that everything is able to "be like God." There was a time when the angel, Lucifer, lived in the holiness of Heaven. He was beautiful and was able to worship God like no other.[4] But in an unthinkable act, he decided to flip the magnet of mirroring God to instead "be like God" in an unholy switch where he now thinks he is God.[5] Then with this twisted and repelling magnetism, he convinced one third of the holy angels of Heaven that they also wanted to flip and "be like God."

Now there are two understandings to this. First, "be like God" is to reflect God's actions and mirror His holiness, and second, "be like God" is to want to actually be God. The latter of the two is a great sin and is why satan and the other rebellious angels were cast out of Heaven. A new place, hell, was created for their rebellion.[6] They are no longer the holy angels of Heaven, but rather they became demons of hell. The mutiny was unthinkable and shocking! The Kingdom of God is unattainable to these demons in the same way that magnets fighting each other cannot connect.

At the beginning of earthly time, when God dwelled with men, He taught Adam and Eve many things about Himself, and there was a wonderful unity between God and mankind. God Himself was sharing His nature so that we could mirror Him.[7] If we were magnets, we were tightly fit to God. Then satan came along and convinced Adam and Eve that they wanted to "be like God" in the way that did not mirror God with love and obedience but with selfish desire.[8] This great sin changed *everything!* We left our holy place of being an object of affection close to God and became His enemies in sin. The Kingdom of God became unattainable to mankind.

Satan knew exactly what would happen when he tempted Adam and Eve to leave the mirror image of God because it had already caused him to be cast out of Heaven. Mankind was now separated from God, and in a twisted way this brought satan pleasure because it hurt God. This is the first foundational sin that changed the course of human history. I will call it the terrible fall, yet many of us have never even considered it because we are born into this despair.[9] The huge chasm of separation between Heaven and earth could not be united. We were lost. The pain of this reality should cause us all to shudder in our spirit. There is, however, a way to bring the Kingdom of Heaven to earth.

RESTORATION

The Trinity (Father, Son, and Holy Spirit) had great love for mankind and created a solution that has been called many things from glorious to scandalous.[10] Jesus, the only son of the Father, would become the God/Man making a way for mankind to be reunited with the Kingdom of God.[11]

In the plan, Jesus would leave His position in Heaven to become a man.[12] We cannot comprehend this.[13] Imagine for a moment leaving humanity to forever become a fish. I realize it sounds silly, but can you imagine being God and leaving Heaven to become man? Inconceivable! Not only would Jesus become a man, but He would live an absolutely sinless life. This is something that no one has ever done, except for Jesus. Then, as the slain Lamb of God, He would die not just a regular death, but a horrific one.[14] This plan would allow Jesus to become a bridge to bring Heaven and men together again.[15] When we look at Jesus dying for us, we should feel indebted to Him and have eternal gratitude.[16] Who would ever do this for countless enemies who may never appreciate it?[17] But there is so much more than the death of Jesus seen clearly in Heaven.[18] In fact, it is His life that bridged the chasm between God and men and restored access to Heaven.[19]

THE KING

There are *many* aspects of Jesus. We will only discuss some individual points and I am only scratching the surface of His attributes!

Jesus is the firstborn from the dead. This means He is the first person who died and gained access to Heaven.[20] Those who died before Jesus did not go to Heaven, but they went to a holding place called Sheol. Jesus became the firstborn of the dead because of how He lived His life as a man. Jesus is known as the second Adam, and He never sinned.[21] Let that sink in.

He mirrored His life for God, in God, with God, and beside God. He lived obediently and sacrificially. What made His death so unthinkable was that Jesus was *without* sin.[22] There was never a separation between Jesus and the Father until Jesus took the weight of our sin and the wrath of God because of the sins of mankind.[23] Before that, magnetically, Jesus was always aligned with His Father. The beholding mirror image of "be like God" was not necessary because He was already God showing us how God mirrors God. In fact, Jesus taught that if we have seen Him, we have also seen the Father.[24] But because He was also one hundred percent man, He was able to mirror God so that believers could now mirror Jesus. He is the perfect example.

Taking the sin of mankind onto His holy self was inconceivable![25] In the magnet analogy, not only would this repel Jesus from the Father, but it would separate the deity of Jesus from His humanity, separating holiness from sin.[26] Supposedly the separation would happen inside of Jesus and destroy Him because that is what sin does—destroys us and separates us. But it was His life of holiness that gave Him the ability to raise Himself from death. The God/Man was not separated from His own deity even though He willingly took the sin of the world and wrapped it around Himself. He proved He is the only One worthy.[27] Because of the holiness within, Jesus was victorious. He made a way for mankind to be with God.[28] Hallelujah!

All of Heaven sees Jesus as the superhero of superheroes. Only one man is worthy in Heaven. Jesus! He is *the* ruler, and no who can ever dethrone Him.[29] He has earned the allegiance of every person ever created because He paid the price for our sin, He went to hell in our stead, and He is the only way to the Father in Heaven still today. His glory is unfathomable, His honor incomparable, and He is forever in the body of a man. He joined mankind back to Heaven. Jesus is the Judge in Heaven, and all of His rulings are perfect and final.[30] He desires, and has desired since the beginning of time, for all people to spend eternity with Him.[31]

CHANGES

The Kingdom changed when Jesus left His throne and became a man. It changed again to accommodate Him in His new identity as both God and Man.[32] This is the Jesus who sits on the throne ruling everything that has ever been created.[33] It is Jesus who welcomes or casts out people depending on each person's personal and magnetic life. In His greatness, Jesus still lets people choose one of the two lifestyles of "be like God." Because He lived and died a man, we have a winning example of how to mirror His life and attain eternity in Heaven.[34]

KINGDOM

Inside of the Kingdom, we find the beginning of the created order and the design of everything that has been created. We can recognize some of the created order here on earth, but there are things in the heavenly Kingdom that are not on the earth. There is a perfect prototype of every created, living thing in Heaven. Think of a redwood tree, crystal clear water, shire horses, or bleeding heart bushes to name just a few things. Everything that is in our world has its perfect "first" in the Kingdom. There are things that God created and placed a replica on the earth, but men destroyed them. Those things are now extinct on earth but not in Heaven. In addition, there are things we can hardly imagine such as angels of every size and design, colors that sing, rocks that are alive, and smells that can satisfy like a three-course meal.

The size of the Kingdom is determined by the spoken words of Jesus. The Kingdom is an everlasting home that will never deplete itself of supernatural resources. The clouds in Heaven stand up in their splendor to give glory to God. In Heaven, everything glorifies the Lord![35] Nothing dies there, and everything communicates with everything else. People communicate with each other heart to heart so that there is never a misunderstanding. People communicate with every created thing in Heaven.

The Kingdom has no darkness, which is not to say there is only daylight.[36] There is a time similar to our night. But it can never be dark because the presence of Jesus is there, and where there is Light, there can be no darkness.[37]

COMMUNITY

The Kingdom is a place of community.[38] Each thing, person, angel, and thought is for the betterment of one another. Sharing, laughing, singing, playing, hugging, and being still together is a lifestyle. The thoughts of God are communicated as if they are individual phone calls. No one is left out of the community gatherings or information downloads. At the same time, no one feels left out of the smaller meetings designed for specific reasons.

Every person who followed Jesus to Heaven has wonderful Christ-esteem instead of self-esteem. The blood of Jesus that was paid for that person, and not their own merit, determines their worth.[39] Moreover, their brightness is determined by their faith and obedience to Jesus while they lived on the earth.

Everything in Heaven makes a song, and we can hear each other's music. Together we make a glorious, harmonious melody.[40] We know each other not only by our sense of sight but by our other senses as well. Each person and thing has brightness, a smell, a taste, and a sound.

A person varies in brightness similar to the stars of the night sky. One may be very bright and stand out, but each one is brilliant against the black sky.[41] Faith through obedience, resolve, and commitment during turmoil and denial of temporal pleasures results in eternal brightness that is an endless mark of one's faithfulness to the King.

CONTROL AND COMPARISON

Control in Heaven is very different. Only the Trinity has majority control. The Lord has made a way in Heaven that is perfect, so there is no need to change anything or try to control. People respectfully and with heartfelt willingness give away all rights of control because they can see His way is perfect. At the same time, free will is never compromised. Each person and thing always has free will. In the Kingdom, we all willingly want Jesus to choose for us. He can never choose incorrectly.

In Heaven there is no comparison. Everyone and everything is strikingly beautiful. We can see what God intended us to see about another person when we look at each other.[42] We are awestruck by the beauty of the one, whichever one, is standing before us. Also, there is no striving to get more. Everyone has more than enough, but it is realized in the heart instead of in materialism. In Heaven, we truly celebrate the good things that someone else has without feeling an ache if we ourselves do not have it. The flipside is that no one is ever embarrassed of having too much because the One who gave it makes everyone exceptional.

In Heaven there are no misunderstandings. Hearts communicate with each other, and because we are sanctified in the Blood of Jesus we are the perfect example of ourselves and are free of all the negatives such as jealousy, malice, hatred, and anger.

THRONE ROOM

The throne room in Heaven is wherever the throne is. It moves from place to place making whichever room it is in the Throne Room. The closest explanation I have is of an elevator. As the elevator moves from floor to floor it is part of that floor while it is there. Similarly, the Throne Room is prepared on different levels, and when the King arrives on His throne, the room is then fully equipped. There are different rooms for different needs. Think about a courthouse and all the different courts and judges that reside there. For instance, there are courts for small claims, civil trial, divorce, criminal trials, abused and neglected children, traffic, etc. Each room is set for different reasons. This is true in Heaven as well. The Throne moves with the only Judge, Jesus.

There is also a wonderful room there where everyone will gather together. I believe this room will be a room of awards. It has a floor that appears like glass. Each of us will be given a crown and accolades for the lives we lived on earth.[43] This room is set for an amazing and glorious time.

There is another room where Jesus hears the prayers of the saints, and another exists where He commissions His holy angels to do His bidding. There is still yet a terrifying room where people who will be cast into hell enter. These people will never see the room with the sea of glass.

HEAVEN BREAKS IN

People see and experience angels every day.[44] In fact, Heaven is always watching and breaking in to situations on the earth to aid people in distress. Sometimes when we have an angelic encounter, we know it immediately, but often we do not realize we were with angels until the situation is over.

This happened for me when our oldest daughter was just an infant. It was before I knew Jesus as my Savior. One evening I was heating up her bottle on the stove. She screamed in my arms as I reached to remove the bottle from the pan. Unfortunately, the water was at a full boil and I realized that the bottle would be too hot. Because I was afraid that the scalding water might drop on her, I swung her to my right side, holding her with only my right arm. As I was repositioning her, she kicked off of me. I immediately dropped the bottle and tried to reposition my left hand to catch her, but I was too late. She fell out of my arms and hit her head on the floor.

She stopped screaming instantly. I did not hesitate. I scooped her up and grabbed the car keys. My husband, Mike, and I rushed her to the emergency room. She did not begin to scream again until the doctor was examining her. He felt that she would be fine, but I did not. I demanded to see a pediatrician. The emergency room doctor felt that I was overreacting, but I held my ground. The pediatrician looked at her and quickly referred us to a hospital two hours away. She was concerned our daughter had severe brain trauma.

There was a terrible snowstorm that night so the Life Flight helicopter could not be used. Instead they ushered us into an ambulance; Mike followed in our car. As we traveled through the snowstorm, we had to stop several times to stabilize our baby girl. Each time Mike feared the worst. It was agony.

When we arrived at the hospital, there were police officers waiting to handcuff me for child abuse. The situation went from bad to worse!

As luck would have it (being lost we only believed in luck), there was a pediatric brain surgeon who had been holding classes at the hospital. He had been informed and was waiting for us to arrive. As soon as he looked at our baby, he told the officers that our little girl needed her mother. The police left with an understanding that the hospital would notify them when needed.

After that, things moved very quickly. The doctor asked me to hold my daughter tightly against my chest to help calm her. I watched as the doctor stuck a needle with a large syringe into the top of her head and began drawing liquid off of her brain. It was unprecedented that they would do this procedure with my daughter in my arms, but he was fighting for her life. I shook with fear. I was distraught and terrified that I wouldn't be able to hold her still enough.

Once the doctor extracted two vials full of liquid, they placed her in a crib. She was strapped down in several places, including her head, to keep her still. Then they cut off her clothes, inserted an IV, and attached numerous monitoring gadgets to her little body. She screamed and cried uncontrollably the entire time.

Then she stopped crying abruptly. They assured me that she was exhausted and only sleeping. It all seemed like a terrible nightmare.

The doctor explained to Mike and me that her situation was dire. I was filled with great sorrow because I felt responsible. Mike could not console me. In my heart of hearts, I believed that she would die and that Mike would never forgive me.

The nurse could see my pain and suggested that maybe I would want to go to the chapel. Quickly following her directions, I took the elevator down to the basement, got off, and turned left. The chapel was a little way down on the right.

It was a small room with a few rows of chairs, but I was the only one there. At the front were two kneeling benches. I chose the one on the right side of the room and I knelt down. However, in my panic and desperation, I had no idea what to do.

Then I noticed a loud clicking sound as a person walked down the corridor I had just exited. The clicking sound was like a woman walking with only one high heel. As the sound entered the room, I turned to see an elderly man walking with a metal-tipped cane. He sat down in the front row.

He was not even attempting to be quiet. I was annoyed that he was in the room. Didn't he know that I was there first?

I turned back around feeling agitated. All of a sudden, whack! I stood quickly and turned around to see the old man standing behind me. He hit my right arm with his cane!

He asked me, *"What are you doing here?"*

In all of my panic and desperation I yelled at him, *"Not that it is any of your business, but my baby is upstairs dying!"*

To which he asked again, more calmly, *"What are you doing here?"*

I couldn't stop the onslaught of tears that were escaping my eyes. I answered, *"I need God to help me!"*

He then said, *"You are not asking correctly."*

My anger was boiling but it did not faze him.

He knelt down on the bench and motioned for me to join him. He asked if I knew how to talk to God. I didn't understand about talking to God but I responded that I knew the Lord's Prayer. He said that was a very good place to start.

I prayed the Lord's Prayer and waited. He told me to do it again. So I did. He placed his hand over my hand and repeated the prayer with me numerous times. His lack of concern or panic and his strength was a great comfort to me.

When he finally spoke again, it was very quiet, *"He is listening; ask Him for what you need."*

I had never asked God for anything so critical up to this point. But the elderly man had helped me get to a place where I was able to approach God. In that moment, I had a knowing inside about the power of who I was talking to—God. I knew that if He answered me, His Kingdom would come on the earth. I knew that if He forgave me for what I considered the biggest mistake of my life, my daughter would be OK. I knew that I needed *Him* to help my daughter!

I am sure my words were unintelligible. I cried harder than I had ever cried before. The man placed his hand on my back and somehow it helped me to ask completely. All of the pain, regret, worry, and desire for my daughter to be healed came rushing out in great sobs. I asked God to heal my baby.

In an instant, I felt the truth of God's answer come to me. I just *knew* that God had heard me and that our daughter was going to be perfectly fine! My weeping turned to great joy!

I quickly stood up to hug the man, but he was gone. I looked around and he was not in the room. I ran down the hallway to the elevator but found that it was still on the basement floor. I returned to the chapel and looked to see if there was a restroom he might have entered. There was not.

Excitedly, I ran back to the elevator and hurried to our daughter's room. As I entered, I saw Mike standing beside the crib just watching her. I rushed over and hugged him.

I told Mike about my encounter with the old man and how he had helped me talk to God. I was so excited to report that God had heard me and was going to fix *everything!* Mike did not understand so I started at the beginning. I explained to Mike that I had prayed the Lord's Prayer at least 50 times until I had finally felt God. I shared that then I knew I had been with Him and that He had listened. I told Mike that God had let me know that He was going to fix our baby as if she had never fallen. Mike was not as certain as I was. But I knew—I could even still feel the bruise on my right arm from where the man had whacked me with his cane.

In a few hours, the pediatrician came to check on our daughter and reported that everything was good. Actually, it was perfect. The hospital was not sure what to do when all of her tests came back normal. They removed all the gadgets attached to her body, fed her, and then she drifted peacefully back to sleep. The doctor said that we were lucky. I explained that God had fixed her. They sent us home with a special helmet for her, just in case.

Heaven broke in for my daughter! It happens all time for people—both lost and saved. When I got saved, the Holy Spirit reminded me of this event and many others where God had sent help to me. Isn't it crazy that He helps us even when we deny Him? Or make promises that we do not keep?

We have only begun to scratch the surface of the many wonderful heavenly truths there are to know. It is imperative that we remain open to an eternity of discovering more, especially now when we need it the most.

NOTES

1. Revelation 12:10-14

2. Hebrews 4:12, 1 Corinthians 2:6-13

3. Isaiah 57:15

4. Ezekiel 28:13

5. Isaiah 14:13

6. Matthew 25:41

7. 2 Peter 1:4

8. Genesis 3:5

9. Genesis 3:17

10. John 3:16

11. John 1:14, Colossians 2:9

12. John 10:36

13. Philippians 2:7

14. John 1:29, Revelation 5:6

15. 2 Corinthians 5:21

16. 1 Peter 1:15

17. Romans 5:8

18. Romans 3:23-25

19. 1 Timothy 2:5

20. Colossians 1:18

21. 1 Corinthians 15:45-49

22. 1 John 3:5

23. Romans 5:8-9

24. John 14:9
25. 2 Corinthians 5:21
26. Matthew 27:46
27. Revelation 5:2-9
28. Romans 3:23-24
29. Revelation 17:14
30. 2 Corinthians 5:10
31. Ephesians 1:4
32. 1 Timothy 2:5, Mark 15:39
33. Colossians 1:16, Revelation 3:21
34. 1 Peter 2:21
35. Psalm 19:1
36. Revelation 22:5
37. 1 John 1:5
38. Revelation 21:3
39. Ephesians 2:8
40. Psalm 148:1-14
41. Daniel 12:3
42. Genesis 1:27
43. Revelation 2:10
44. Hebrews 13:2

CHAPTER 5

THE OVEN TIMERS

"Give us this day our daily bread."

—MATTHEW 6:11

The Bread of Life is baked in Heaven's kitchen. Before I tell you about the bread, let me explain what I believe led up to this encounter.

God has made me a seer with the heart of an evangelist. Or maybe I am an evangelist who is also a seer. The Bible teaches that a prophet has eyes to see but a seer has all the senses in addition to sight—sound, taste, smell, and touch.[1] This allows the seer's prophecies to move in a stronger discernment. Also, a seer is most accurate at "feeling" not only their emotions, but also the emotions everyone around them.

I see things that cause me to know that I must warn people of a day that is coming when it will be imperative that we have made the right choice. We each must choose Jesus in our lifetime, or we will spend eternity without Him. On the day that each one stands before God, and none of us know the day, every person will bow their knees and confess that He is Lord.[2] If we did not choose Him before that day, He will tell us that our choice demands that we depart.[3]

Do you know anyone who has died unexpectedly? My brother died suddenly. It was terrible! Nothing prepared us for that day. In an instant, everything changed. There was no more time to share the truth of Jesus. My last words to him are unchangeable. Thankfully for my personal sanity, in that split second between life and death, I reminded my brother to call on God.

Everyone dies, but where we spend eternity can bring great peace or terrible torment.[4] We don't know how much time we have or how much time anyone has. Keeping that reality of time in our hearts helps us be bold and say everything Jesus wants us to say in any given moment. Realistically, *you* may be the last person who shares the good news about Jesus with someone before they die. Or you may be the person God was counting on who didn't.

Let me explain what was happening in the days leading up to this vision. I went to a store to pick up a big order for a large water baptism our church was doing. I had special ordered over 300 towels. While I waited for the customer service people to collect the order, I walked around their store. I noticed a woman shopping in the infant section, and I was drawn to her. I knew it was the Holy

Spirit.[5] We talked about how cute the baby clothes are nowadays. I told her about my grandbabies and how grateful I am to God for choosing me as their grandmother. She explained that the subject of God is a touchy subject, and she only talks about Him with safe people. I told her how I would greatly enjoy hearing about her relationship with God.

She answered, *"Well, I go to a church that accepts me."*

I said, *"What kind of church is that, that upsets you?"*

She said, *"No, I didn't say 'upsets,' I said 'accepts.' They accept me."*

I said, *"What's the special need that you have to be accepted?"*

She said, *"I am a lesbian, and I'm very proud of it. Our church accepts many of us."*

I was shocked. I am sure she could see it in my face. I knew I needed to say something hard, so I stopped and internally prayed. Who does she remind me of? This is important because if I think of someone I love and how I would want them approached, I find myself being much gentler and kinder. I will address people with love and care if I take that minute and pray.[6] I reached out for her hand. I gently and as gingerly as possible said, *"Honey...the church might accept you, but Heaven can't accept you in blatant sin."*

She was instantly in a state of wrath.[7] She wanted nothing to do with me and shoved my hands away.[8] I continued explaining that I did not know what kind of place she attends, but Jesus' Church wants to help all sinners *out* of whatever sinful lifestyle has entangled them. I told her that all sexual immorality is sinful, including sex before marriage, swinging, sharing, swapping, same sex, and having sex with animals.[9] All of it is separating us from Jesus.

She said, *"You are not a Christian because you hate me!"* She felt that I hated her, but that was far from the truth. Just because I didn't agree with her didn't mean that I hated her, any more than agreeing is proof that I love her. I explained how we all need help out of some kind of sin. I told her that the Bible says that all people have sinned and fall short of glory on our own.[10] I offered to help her.

She was so offended! She told me that it was people like me who ruin Christianity. She said that I was like a Pharisee, keeping people from God.[11] I asked her if we could talk more because the last thing I was trying to do was offend her. I offered to take her out for a nice lunch. I asked if I could share how Jesus could set her free. Instead of a conversation, she stormed off.

I began praying that God would help her and that she would encounter the truth.

Suddenly, a manager came up to me inquiring if I had harassed a customer in this area. The manager said that the customer was so hurt and upset that she couldn't stop crying about how mean someone had been to her. I told the manager that whoever she was looking for couldn't be me. I hadn't been mean to anyone. The manager asked me if I had told a lesbian woman that God hated her and that Heaven would not accept her. Well, only part of that was true. I did not tell her that God hated her.

The manager asked me to leave her store as she began walking me to the door. I replayed the conversation for her. I proceeded to explain that I am a Christian and as such I had to tell the other customer the truth with love. The manager said that she also was a

Christian. However, instead of agreeing with the scripture, she said that she would not tolerate people like me hurting other people. She stated that "her" Jesus wanted us to love others, not threaten them. She tried pushing tolerance and human understanding as the gospel. She didn't care what the Bible said, only what she felt.

I told her that God does not tolerate sin. She disagreed. I asked the manager if we should tell people who are drinking poison that it could kill them? She was not willing to engage with me as she felt that I was old-fashioned in taking the Bible literally. She told me that she has family members in the homosexual lifestyle and that she knew that they would go to Heaven. I asked her how she knew this. She just became angrier.

As we neared the front of the store, I asked if I could stop and purchase the large order of towels that was waiting. She immediately changed her tune and told me to go ahead and finish my shopping. She said that she was sorry she mistook me for a radical solicitor and suggested that I look up all the ways Jesus is tolerant and understanding. Then she misquoted the Bible to me, saying that Jesus desires mercy more than sacrifice.[12] I asked her to look at the passage in its context because she was misusing it. She walked away as if I had not spoken.

For many days afterward, the interactions from that day deeply bothered me. In addition, the enemy was using the incident to beat me up. The devil comes after me for being a witness who shares the love and truth of Jesus. Sometimes he is unrelenting in the discouragement.

We can't afford to be cute with our words or tell only half-truths.[13] God will hold us accountable for what we say, but also for what we do not. Telling that lesbian woman the truth according to God was love. I tried to remember if I had been gentle while being firm. It was the sin inside her that didn't like me telling her that Heaven wouldn't accept her. It was the enemy who didn't want her to feel conviction, which results in change. *We all have to change.*[14] We all have to come under the authority of Jesus Christ. Heaven is His home, His Kingdom. Our God is amazing and forgives sins. But He doesn't allow blatant disrespect and dishonor. I was extremely confused by the manager's actions and reactions to both the lesbian woman and me.

When we stand before Jesus, we will not spend time telling Him what happened because He already knows everything. If we are not welcomed, then we will depart.[15] As Christians, we know this. It is the love of God that compels us to warn others, or it is lovelessness and fear of man that keeps us silent.

The negative thoughts kept bombarding my mind: *"You weren't nice enough! You misunderstood her! You should have dialed down! Now she's never going to go to Heaven because of you!"*

This was the state of turmoil that I felt. I was filled with worry and doubt.

My prayers were, *"God, did I do this all wrong? Lord, can You forgive me?"*

After a week of this mental stress, I went to be by myself and parked my car so that I could look at the water of a nearby lake. All of a sudden, I was in Heaven. I was in the kitchen. But it was not like any of our kitchens. It was amazing! It was huge!

By the size of the room, I could tell they did a lot of cooking there. Everyone was busy baking bread. My grandmother used to make homemade bread when I was a child. I love everything to do with baking bread—the smell, the taste, the melted butter on top, the salt, and definitely the satisfaction of eating it. It was always so yummy and a personal favorite!

The angels working in the kitchen weren't wearing their wings. They were *big*, happy, laughing, and telling stories about the amazing things Jesus had done. Jesus was also there, laughing with His angels. Jesus likes to have fun. They were telling funny stories of remarkable events in the times before time. The Lord said, *"I remember that!"* and He laughed. He loves to laugh. When He laughs, His joy leaves His body and goes inside of the people around Him. Everyone else was laughing at the joke the Lord had made when He said that He remembers. He never forgets, unless it is under His blood.

Have you ever been on a hilly, gravel country road? If you go really fast over the hills, it can cause your belly to bounce and that tickle in your tummy can take your breath away. That's what His laugh does. It creates a remarkable fun that makes us *want* to be around Him. Our God likes to play with us. When we get to Heaven, we will be very happy to have childlikeness. Our bodies won't hurt anymore.[16] We will be able to do amazing things and finally be invincible. We will think like children again, believing with simple faith.

In the heavenly kitchen, Jesus was telling wonderful things about a particular angel, and everyone laughed out of the pure joy of hearing God explain all the wonderful quirky qualities He had created and placed inside of that angel, making the angel *perfect!* I enjoyed listening and laughing with them. There was one angel who laughed so wonderfully that we all laughed along with him. In no time, we were all belly laughing. Everybody is capable of doing belly laughs in Heaven. It was just so much fun and afterward I felt so relaxed. Then, because it was contagious, somebody would get us going again.

They were laughing so hard they couldn't even tell the rest of the story. Even though they had already heard the story, they loved hearing it again and celebrating each other. It was amazing to be in a place where others shared good and wonderful things, and everyone wanted to listen and laugh together.

I was in the bakery part of the kitchen that was very large and tall. I remember thinking that this is where they made the manna that God sent down to the earth during the exodus.[17] No one told me this, but in Heaven we know things aplenty from God-given knowledge and wisdom.

One whole wall of the kitchen was the oven, covered with doors from floor to ceiling and spanning across the entire wall. The angels could open each oven door individually and slide out a tray.

The oven was a heavenly engineering miracle. If I could have walked around the wall, it was about a foot deep. However, the tray holding the bread was at least eight feet long. (Side note: it is common in Heaven to think, *"How did they do that?"* They can do lots of things there because it is Heaven.) Inside of each oven door was a loaf of the Lord's bread for the people on the earth. The laughing turned into squeals of joy and excitement because the timers were all going off and the bread was finally ready.

Jesus desires to give us bread every single day.[18] He wants to feed us good things each day. His bread revives good memories and dreams that He is looking forward to for us. This bread is also something that gives substance and guidance and has amazing properties to heal. The angels were baking this bread for the multitudes—for every tongue, tribe, and people group on earth.

I was brought to Heaven on this occasion to be one of the Lord's servants who would take His gift of daily bread to the people on earth. I didn't know what I should do or how to bring it.

Jesus was standing beside me and said, *"What do you think?"*

I said, *"I don't know what to think."*

He said, *"You're a worker of the harvest."*[19]

I was so happy to agree. *"Oh yes, Lord, I am!"* I've always wanted to be one of His workers!

The angels were taking out all the bread, and it was *amazing!* The smell was so intoxicating. It smelled so much better than my grandmother's bread. My first thought was about eating it. My second thought was that I had never tasted the bread in Heaven, and I just knew it would be much better than any kind I had ever tried.

I turned around to look at all the piles of bread. It was finally ready to go, but there were no other workers waiting. I wondered why there were so few workers. It was upsetting. This wonderful gift was prepared specifically with the precise recipe of the Lord and made especially for the people on the earth. I looked at the wall oven again. There were maybe a hundred doors, each producing a long bundle of bread, and I was the only worker there?

I felt mixed emotions. I was excited to be there as a worker, but at the same time, I felt overwhelmed because there was too much work for just me. All of the loaves needed to be delivered. The angels started handing me bread. They gave me the first loaf of bread, a big long log. Wow! It was more remarkable than I can explain. This bread was meaty and very dense. They piled three on me and I was doing everything I could to hold on to those massive loaves.

I was excited! I had food from God for people! I looked over at Jesus, and He said, *"You can do this! Tell them, 'Eat the bread!'"*

In Heaven when He says you can do it, you believe you can do it. Then when you are not in Heaven you think, *"Why did I think I could do it?"* But while I was in front of Him, I knew I could. He told me to repeat the words. Repeating them gave me an awesome advantage that I did not have previously. (Always repeat what Jesus says, and you will have that same advantage.) The Lord pointed for me to go through the door on the far end of the oven wall. I was trying to figure out how I would get the long bread through that door. The Lord knew my thoughts and told me to just keep walking. To be obedient, I kept my eyes closed because in my own understanding there was no way I could get through the door.[20]

Somehow, the bread made it through the wall with me and I was now in a different place. I was at a church on the earth. The people at the church were in a worship service. I was so excited, and I knew exactly what to do! As I looked at the loaf of bread I was carrying, I saw that it was large but manageable. It was not like the one I had in Heaven, and now I only had one loaf with me.

I yelled, *"Hey everybody! Guess what? God sent bread! There's enough for all of us! Come and taste it!"*

They said, *"We don't want that bread! We don't know what's in it or where it was made. We eat the bread of tolerance and understanding."*[21]

They were making many excuses and talked badly about the gift. They said that the bread I carried would exclude people and make people change. I was shocked. I quickly became worried and started crying because God sent bread but nobody wanted to eat it. I knew the timing of this bread was for right now. It wasn't going to be any good tomorrow. I remembered the exact words that the Lord had said, and I had not yet said them. I tried to get their attention again, but they wouldn't listen.[22]

I yelled, *"Eat the bread!"* but no one did. I said it again and again to no avail.

I was so sad! I started to eat the center of the bread. Then the people began mocking me.[23] They didn't need this old-fashioned bread because they had new bread of tolerance and understanding.

I yelled through my tears, *"That kind of bread is poison!"*

Again I told them the words of the Lord, *"Eat the bread!"*

All of a sudden, that loaf of bread disappeared. I was broken-hearted that the people would not try the bread. They would not be sustained in an hour of need. Instead, they were eating poison.

In an instant, I was moved to an area where I was with friends, family, co-workers, and acquaintances. I was holding the second loaf of bread. Once more, I was very excited because I knew these people. I was calling them by name, *"Look! Look! God loves us! He gave me bread to give to you!"*

Again, this group of people were not interested. They were offended that God had given the bread to me. *"Why did He give it to you? God wouldn't give it to you!"*

I answered that it didn't matter that He gave it to me because it was for them.[24] But the people ignored me and went back to their tasks.

I remembered His words so I called out, *"Eat the bread!"* But no one did.

They told me that they like to eat the bread of "tolerance and understanding." They did not believe that God would send bread from Heaven or that the bread I was holding was from there. I didn't know what to do. I looked at the gift that the Lord had sent, and I started eating it. I was crying again because I knew God had a special purpose for this bread to help us, nourish us, and strengthen us. He had something planned, but this group would not receive it either. I felt terrible. I didn't know what to do as a worker of the harvest. The bread disappeared, and I moved locations again.

I was now in an unknown area, and it was dark outside. I sensed that it was a dangerous place. There was an old burn barrel with a fire surrounded by homeless people trying to warm their hands. I knew that society would call them the unwanted, the dirty, the problems, or the "less than" people. These were the people who get passed day by day, like the people who live under the bridges, on the street corners begging for money, or picking through the garbage.

Before I could say anything, they all started coming toward me. They could smell the hot bread I was carrying. They were coming forward from out of the darkness to join me at the fire barrel. I begin telling them, *"Jesus has sent you a gift! Eat the bread!"*[25]

They couldn't believe that it was free. The first lady said that they usually only eat the bread of tolerance and understanding but that she discovered that it is a poison. She ripped off a huge chunk of the bread in my arms. Then, she quickly ripped another, handing it to the person behind her. Other people came up and also started ripping off the ends of the loaf. They were so thankful!

They kept saying, *"Thank you for bringing this bread!"*[26]

They were calling to others in the darkness, *"Eat the bread!"* There were so many people. I talked to each new group about how much Jesus loves them and how He wants to clean us all up so that we can be with Him forever in Heaven. One man broke my bread in half and went a distance off and began feeding more people.

They wanted me to tell them more. Instead of the bread disappearing, it became larger and began looking like the loaf from Heaven. It seemed that the more I told them stories about the goodness of Jesus, the more people came. I shared how we all need to be set free from our sins. I preached to the crowds on holiness and sanctification.[27] Everyone was hungry to listen and to change.

And you know what? They all wanted the bread. They would rip off a piece and hand it to somebody else. *"Here, did you get some?"* And they checked on one another, yelling out, *"Eat the bread!"* That was when I realized that by eating the bread, we had two strengths. First, we gained the knowledge of what to change, and second, we had the strength to make the change.

The longer I stood there, the more people came! The smell of the bread was becoming like the smells in Heaven, almost overwhelming! Somehow that smell was filling the streets and bringing people from everywhere. Shortly, other people who had been there were now telling about the bread. They were confessing how powerful it is to be filled up with food from God. They began preaching about needing to be right with God. It felt like all the people were eating the bread and heading out to get others who were too far away and who might not know about the bread. And all the while, the pieces of bread kept getting bigger!

Then out of nowhere, someone got healed! As soon as this happened, we all began yelling, *"Eat the bread!"* Unprecedented numbers of people were coming and ripping off pieces of the bread. Children were getting chunks from the underside, others were ripping it from the ends and the middle, and yet it grew and smelled sweeter. After eating a few bites, people began saying, *"Tell us about Jesus!"*

I understood this was supposed to happen. When we bring the truth of the gospel, in the minute that we're providing it, it should be like fresh, hot bread especially made just for that person. The people eating it enjoyed it in such a way that they fell in love with it much like I had with my grandmother's bread. Of course, you would want to share it with someone else.[28]

I was so happy that I had been a worker of the harvest, and I was positive that we had used up at least those 100 loaves that were made in Heaven. I was also sure that the timers must be sounding again, and the angels would be sending more bread. The Lord's plan was successful. More than that, the plan was life-giving and sustaining!

I began singing a song about the bread of life. *"Eat, eat, eat the bread. Eat the bread the Master made. Eat, eat, eat the bread. It will accomplish all He'd prayed."* Then others started singing about the bread. It was a most wonderful time!

After this vision, I sat and asked God about the kitchen in Heaven and the bread. I did a lot of thinking on the lessons He desires for us to know. He is still teaching me from that visit. When I pray, "give me this day my daily bread,"[29] I am asking for a lot! I am asking for the special bread from Heaven. I believe we are asking for the gospel and ultimately the *Man* who is the Bread of Life.[30]

The thing about the gospel is that we can't change its truths. We can't decide that love is changing what the Bible says because people are offended by the way God wants things. If we do, then we think we are more compassionate than God. We can't change the truth because we think that the way it is might make people feel bad. The bread the Lord has sent is the right bread, the nourishing word. The bread from Heaven helps us, strengthens us, and causes us to want to share it with others.

In that vision of Heaven, bread was made every day. His angels were working very hard, and I wish there had been more workers of the harvest lined up. It's sad to know that the timers are all going off but there are very few people willing to do that service for Jesus—a service that takes His truth to the world.

Not all churches are like the church I encountered in the vision. It is the Church that shows us how to become a worker and to accept the truths from the Bible. The Church is not tolerant of sin and desires obedience to the instructions of the Bible. The Bible says that God's Church is supposed to prevail over the gates of hell.[31] This is the kind of church we want to become. We want to be a body of *workers!* Even if the church we are trying to serve doesn't want the bread, we still have to take it there. Jesus still wants His bread to go to them. You don't know—maybe somebody there will eat the bread and start talking, and then everybody will want to eat the bread.

Additionally, we must continue bringing the bread to our families, friends, co-workers, and acquaintances, even if in our explanation we seem intolerant. We know the bread of tolerance is death. We must adhere to *God's* standard even if no one else eats the bread with us. It's true that these people know us; but if we keep bringing that same bread, again and again, in truth and in love, the smell will eventually entice them. Maybe not the first time, but we can't grow weary doing this good work.[32] Maybe it's going to take a thousand times of bringing the gift before anyone will try it. In the end, you will be so glad that you kept trying.

I have no idea how many times the Lord sent bread for me, and I refused. I must eat the bread too. Jesus is sending it for everyone, and He won't quit. That's who He is—a God who remembers the reasons why He put quirky qualities inside of each of us. He remembers that He made us to laugh and deeply desires to belly laugh in Heaven with each of us.

When we get to Heaven, we're going to have so many stories to tell of great things that God did because we let Him feed us. The angels will be there, and we will be blissful.

I have prayed about the bread that He is sending for me. I believe sometimes the bread He sends is a correcting kind. I need correction, and the Bible says that He corrects those He loves.[33] I don't want to go off in the wrong direction and eat the bread of tolerance and understanding as if I am more compassionate than Jesus. Eating that bread will definitely let sin carry me away. I would hope someone would love me or love Jesus enough to help me by telling me the whole truth.

Sometimes when I eat the bread from Heaven, I'm just downright hungry. I've spent all the energy I had, and I need more. Other times, I need to eat the bread because I must believe God more. Regardless of the reason, I need to eat the bread that He sends!

As a worker of the harvest, I need to be able to take what is prepared to the people because the timers in Heaven are going off and the timers of the breath of our lives are also going off. The question is: are we willing?

I want to go to the kitchen in Heaven every day. I want to have equipped arms that allow me to carry more of the bread because it is only going to last so long. Our time to share the truth of God will only last so long.

One day, in the near future, the ovens of Heaven will make a different kind of bread. It will be the bread served at the Wedding of the Lamb. Only the people who have eaten from the Bread of Life made during times we are in now will be able to attend that banquet in Heaven. If people haven't eaten from the bread of life, if they don't know Jesus Christ yet, they won't make it to the wedding of the Lamb. That's where we come in.

I still share the truth of Jesus Christ. Frequently, I share it with atheists, agnostics, or people who went to church as a child. I talk to them about the hunger created in us for the bread of Heaven. I oftentimes cry after the encounter because they were not willing or able to accept the bread. I explain that there is counterfeit bread called tolerance and understanding, but in realty it is poison.

At times, when I reach out with the truth of Jesus, it is quickly accepted and produces the changes that God desires. I will not be discouraged to despair; instead, I will keep listening spiritually for the timers to go off so that I can tell others to *"Eat the bread!"*[34]

NOTES

1. Isaiah 29:10
2. Romans 14:11
3. Matthew 7:23
4. Hebrews 9:27
5. John 14:26
6. 1 Peter 3:15

7.   Colossians 3:6

8.   2 Timothy 4:3

9.   Matthew 15:19-20, 1 Corinthians 6:9-11

10. Romans 3:23

11. Matthew 23:13

12. Matthew 9:13

13. Jude 1:23

14. 2 Corinthians 5:14

15. Matthew 7:23

16. Revelation 21:4

17. Exodus 16, Numbers 11:7

18. Matthew 6:11

19. Matthew 9:37-38

20. Proverbs 3:4-5

21. Romans 1:23

22. Matthew 13:15

23. 2 Peter 3:3

24. Acts 24:16

25. Isaiah 55:1

26. Mark 8:6

27. Hebrews 12:14

28. Luke 14:23

29. Matthew 6:11

30. John 6:32-33

31. Matthew 16:18

32. Galatians 6:9

33. Hebrews 12:6

34. Galatians 6:9

CHAPTER 6

---✦◆✦---

ANCIENT COMMUNICATION

"And one said unto him, Lord, are they few that are saved? And he said unto them, Strive to enter in by the narrow door: for many, I say unto you, shall seek to enter in, and shall not be able."

—LUKE 13:23-24 ASV

In another Heaven encounter, I was sitting on a courtroom bench beside the Father. As the presence of God pressed on me, I received a small bit of His knowledge.[1] The first thing I realized is that He is perfect wisdom; He knows everything. The second thing I realized is that everything about God is alive.[2] Nothing can die around Him. He is life forevermore, and I felt so alive! Here on the earth everything is dying, but in Heaven we go from glory to glory and life to life.[3] It sounds presumptuous to say that I was right where I belonged, but the Creator desires for us to understand how things are when everything is right. With Him, everything is right and righteous. Apart from Him, we die.

One thing I noticed right away was that I really liked myself, no...loved myself. Beside Him, I understood that I am just as I should be, just as He created.[4] I was able to agree with Him in things that might otherwise be difficult. For instance, I loved the shape of my chin, the sound of my voice, and the way I laugh. Being with Him, I fit perfectly in my own skin with no desire to change things about myself. In Heaven, I am perfect because there are no comparisons from His heart about me. I'm very special! God thinks that my life is worth the blood of the slain Lamb.[5] As I write these words, I am refreshed and overcome with my importance to God.

Snuggled beside Him, I knew His thoughts toward me, and they instilled confidence that was liberating and freeing. His thoughts toward me were 100 percent responsible for the wonderful acceptance I felt for myself.

The bench we were on was barrel-shaped. It was made of an ancient wood that was emitting light. As I ran my hand on it, I was excited because I knew it was alive. I also knew that this wood was from the time before the terrible fall. When I touched the wood, I knew its story. All trees before the terrible fall were like this, filled with a penetrating light that made them transparent. In that time, everything carried the light of Jesus, the creation light that comes from the heart of the Father.[6] The light flowed through the tree like sap. Even though it was a bench, it was alive. The trees on the earth used to be like that. Heaven has always carried this brilliant, penetrating light. However, at the fall, even the trees were changed and they lost their ability to be seen as glass-like.[7] When sin entered the world with Adam and Eve's choice, everything changed. It was a terrible, painful fall for all of creation! Since that time, everything groans and is in need of healing.[8] Today we cannot see the need for healing because we don't know what creation looked like before sin.

The room we occupied had a most ancient feel to it as well. This room was a place for sharing with God. It was a place of help and hope where men's petitions and prayers were heard and answered. It was a room for men to draw near to God and share the depths of the human heart.[9] For lack of a better understanding, it was a room of ancient communication. This place was untouched by the terrible fall.

The Judge's bench was surrounded by a white glow that I knew was "the Fear-of-the-Lord." Depending on who was gazing at the cloud, it was either a magnifying glass or a hindrance to seeing the Man on the seat. The Fear-of-the-Lord is the beginning of wisdom.[10] It is a necessity to connect to the Man on His bench. The more desire one has for the Fear-of-the-Lord, the more our capacity is opened for understanding. In other words, coming with no Fear-of-the-Lord is defiance, whereas coming with the Fear-of-the-Lord shows Him we are trying and allows Him to help us.

The Man sitting on that bench was by far the most impressive light in the room.[11] He is the Ancient of Days.[12] This man knew everything. He knew the first second of time and each one since. Even now, He experiences life during the times before time. There is no one who compares to this great God!

I have talked with people who believe that they have lived many lives. This is untrue, and they are deceived! We exist because the Father's ancient heart longed to create us. His desire is what knit me and formed me in my mother's womb.[13] Before I was born into this sin-filled world, I was a perfect example of His amazing light. He desires for us to be with Him always. The terrible fall changed everything. Not only did it steal this light, but it also attacked the idea that God gives only one life to each creation. Additionally, the fall polluted the truth of His absolute supremacy over all false gods and suggested that we could have wisdom apart from Him.

I sat on the bench, not realizing it was His throne. When Father God decided or granted a request, it was finished, and there was no appeal process. Thus, it was not only a bench but also a throne. I could see through the Fear-of-the-Lord cloud because I was seated on the bench with the One who made it. I could see from the inner courts to the outer courts. There were massive stairways leading up to the chamber where we were. The entrance between the inner and outer courts was a massive, heavy archway set atop pillars made of the same ancient, transparent, light-filled, living wood as the bench. The structure itself was an architectural miracle. The archway stood there because the Lord had spoken it that way when He created it. As I looked at the pillars, I realized that they were trees—the same type of tree as the bench where we sat.

There was an ancient inscription written on the archway. I could not read the language but knew it was about the absolute, unchanging Ancient of Days.[14] It was just one word—an explanation of communication before sin. I knew that this communication ability was perfect but rarely used on the earth anymore. Although I am sure my simple words will portray this poorly, I am going to try to explain from my limited memory what I understood perfectly while sitting on the bench.

Before the fall of mankind, people's hearts had an ability to *think*. Our hearts beat to the same love-beat that is in our great God. Adam and Eve's hearts had an ability to think, react, feel, express, and be like God's heart. It was a normal act with every beat. Communication with God was a unity that produced the Fear-of-the-Lord. It enabled them to stand in His presence and look into His most beautiful face. After the terrible fall, this communication lost its light, similar to what happened to the trees. We really have no idea the devastation that sin brought and still brings! This gift of thinking from our hearts, communicating, was perverted, twisted, and dangerous. The human heart became dark, and sin corrupted communication immediately![15] Adam and Eve could not think with their hearts like God anymore. Their actions proved it—hiding, blaming, covering, mistrusting, disobeying, etc.[16]

I also understood that an accelerated perversion of this communication resulted in the actions God took at the Tower of Babel when He removed the gift of communication.[17] For our own good, He took this ability away. It is true that He separated languages making it difficult to communicate. However, this was not the primary problem. There was now a terrible separation in communicating between the hearts of God and mankind, husbands and wives, parents and children, men and women, people and animals. There was a huge death in communication. Where once men could converse freely, now the veiled heart caused suspicion, mistrust, manipulation, hiddenness, and that ancient communication gift was concealed from men.

In other words, the fall twisted the perfect, harmonious communication between God and men, which then perverted communication between everyone and everything. The Fear-of-the-Lord was not embraced but became an unhealthy "Dread-of-God." Dread-of-God includes unbelief, mistrust, suspicion, and doubt, which caused us to control, manipulate, and distance ourselves from God.

This counterfeit understanding of God convinced people's hearts to believe we did not need God and that He is not good. In fact, it caused us to be afraid of His sovereignty because He gets the final decision for allowing pain and loss in our lives. Left unchecked in its wickedness, it demolished hearts toward each other and, of course, toward God.

The Lord in His mercy restricted this damaged means of communication at the Tower of Babel.[18] Now, only those who desire and cherish the Fear-of-the-Lord can ascend His holy hill, have clean hands and a pure heart, enter His gates with thanksgiving and His courts with praise, and see the truth that the human heart is deceitful above all things and desperately wicked.[19]

The word inscribed on the archway was a treasure that demanded a special response from men in order to begin in the human heart. Those who understood that there was a process to restore communication would begin to climb the stairs in prayer to speak to God.

God waited on His bench to hear the requests of men. From the bottom of the massive stairway, everyone could see the amazing light of the throne. As people's prayers ascended like smoke, so could their footsteps. Some began climbing in prayer, but soon they stalled, stopped, or quit. They thought it was too hard to pray to get into the chamber. However, the process of climbing was an important part of the preparation to better communicate with God.

Everyone who climbed the stairs had to pass under the arch on a special floor. It was like they were weighed as they passed. The weighing was not in pounds but in the condition of their hearts and thoughts. This arch system's walkway evaluated the condition of a person, and the floor showed various degrees of light or no light at all. In other words, the sin in their lives caused the walkway to not light as they passed. Since the terrible fall, righteousness in human hearts was polluted.[20] The person could not inspect their own heart, so the arch and floor system let them see their true spiritual condition compared to the Lord. It both shocked and amazed me! The spiritual light of some believers was brighter than in others, but it was always less brilliant than the Lord's.

As the people passed through the weighing system, they approached the bench. The degree of light shown by the floor determined how close they could come to the Fear-of-the-Lord.

The people coming up the stairs could not see me as I nestled beside the Father, who was snuggling me close. My heart was totally trusting, which caused Him to laugh. It was the wonderful belly laugh, so contagious that everyone does it in Heaven. When He belly laughs, if you don't know Him, the sound could scare the daylights out of you.

I have a friend who is rough, tough, big, and burly. He doesn't try to be intimidating, but he has a deep, loud voice that rumbles when he speaks and he walks heavy like an elephant. He had always intimidated me until the first time I watched his two-year-old granddaughter come to him. She climbed on him with a huge smile, pulled on his beard, and told him how much she loved him. I thought, *"Look at that baby. She sees right through that tough exterior."*

This is like God, whose voice thunders like many waters—it makes Heaven happy when it does.[21] He sounds just like He should, and He is perfect. When we love Him, we look forward to that thunderous sound. Being on His bench with Him and hearing His marvelous, thunderous voice and belly laugh brought me deep comfort. I laid my head down on His lap in perfect peace, not at all intimidated.

All of a sudden, I heard a ruckus. I was startled and began to get up. I thought that if Father was on official business, I should leave.

He said, *"It's OK, stay."*

I sensed that whatever was happening was highly important because He had become quite serious. I watched as a group of men climbed up all the stairs and crossed the amazing walkway. As they did, their sin blocked all light from the weighing system. Although the darkness inside of them was evident, they were not willing to look at the pathway and agree that they were dark. If they had, they would have stopped, repented, and obtained clearer vision of the Fear-of-the-Lord cloud. Even I could tell that these men had ulterior motives.

I understood that the Father was letting me stay to grow my understanding in something. I am a hands-on learner, and He knows this. I slowly stood up and realized just how little I was, like that two-year-old granddaughter in the arms of her grandfather.

I saw that these men were leaders of the Church on earth. They were rushing into the presence of God. They were shaking fists at the throne. I was shocked at how they came in—very demanding! They were using the name of Jesus, but the walkway they stood on did not become brighter, even as they said His name.

One shouted, *"You will answer this prayer!"*

These men had no idea they were actually standing in the presence of God! They had no idea of the contempt and manipulation in their voices as they said the Savior's name. They saw the Fear-of-the-Lord cloud as a hindrance.

The Father was unmoved by their anger, and instead He intently listened.

I was upset! How could they demand without even checking with Him! The presumption of these men was rude! I was getting ready to tell them that they should not talk to the Father that way! My body was rigid, and my fists were clenched. These ones were filled with anger. Seldom is human anger a righteous thing, and mine was not either.[22] Sitting on the bench, I realized that I was only there because of His purpose for me to gain understanding. Nothing inside of me had the right to judge the men or to question God's ways.[23]

As I watched, I understood that the proper protocol was to approach God's presence with love and thanksgiving.[24] These men were not thankful at all. They were angry and impatient. They were filled with presumption. Suddenly I could see that I was just like them, and probably worse because I was inside the circle of the Fear-of-the-Lord. My heart began repenting, with tears streaming from my eyes. I knew that I did not have enough Fear-of-the-Lord.

The men were yelling at the Father because they felt He had not done certain things for them. They were saying things like:

"I demand that the natural line up with the supernatural!"

"I declare and decree that this situation will bow to the will of Jesus," and *"I demand that resources be released, in the name of Jesus."*

Everyone was correcting God in their prayers. They felt that God was not listening. They felt that He did not care because He had not done what they desired in the way they wanted.

Standing in front of Him, with hope deferred, their hearts turned darker.[25] Then they began to curse God. It was shocking.

One shouted, *"How dare You!"*

Oh, the pride we have—the created ones railing against the Creator! I thought about correcting them, only to remember the many times that I have approached God with the same pride in my heart. Suddenly, I was torn in my identity. I liked who I was in His presence, but that was only when my heart beat in unison with the Father so that I was communicating heart to heart as intended.

Instantly the men disappeared, not because the Father had sent them away, but because the pain and darkness that had engulfed their hearts demanded that they leave. Because they did not have the Fear-of-the-Lord, they could not bring their requests before the King. The cloud surrounding the Lord could not be penetrated with anything false.

There was a deep sadness in the chamber. I knew the very bench I sat on felt it. I didn't understand. I lacked wisdom.

I worriedly said, *"Father, why did You let them talk to You like that? Why didn't You remind them who You are? Why didn't You make something shake or break?"*

Many thoughts were going through my head about what He could do to make people honor Him. And there it was, clear as day—my twisted fear, Dread-of-God, coming out.

He said, *"Shhh."*

As He quieted me, I made a choice. I returned to Him with weeping. Often my thoughts are not His thoughts, but they can be.[26] The Bible tells of a time when the Lord's disciples wanted to call down fire on people. Jesus said to them that they didn't know which spirit they were operating from.[27] Obviously, it was not His Spirit!

In my quieted heart, I questioned, *"Why does He let us talk to Him that way?"*

He heard my thoughts and answered, *"I desire you all to be close."*

Silence. There was a deep silence. The King had shown His vulnerability. The people of the earth are His vulnerability! Because of His great longing for us, He would take us any way that we would come. He knew there was still time for them to change their hearts toward Him. Much like the relationship between God and Pharaoh.[28] Where is the respect and honor due the Savior?[29] We are more respectful to a boss, a policeman, even a stranger. And yet, when we approach Him with manipulation and control and ridiculous thoughts, He waits, and reaches for ways to help us hear and understand.

I need to *know* Jesus so much better than I do—the One who shed His holy blood to purchase sinners! I can't believe that the Ancient One would let us come into His presence without the gift of thanksgiving or pure hearts. But then, who could come?[30] This knowledge changed me.

I needed Him to stop my heart and restart it with the gift of communication that allows me to think like Him. The fall twisted the perfect, unified, deep, heart-to-heart communication with the Father. After the Tower of Babel, this communication was broken and veiled because of the people's arrogance. He did this for their protection. Having the Fear-of-the-Lord is the way to re-enter this ancient and unified communication between humans and God. Just like the cloud in the encounter, the Fear-of-the-Lord amplifies or veils our communication with the Lord. Any other way leads to separation and death. In prayer, we must choose to trust, obey, and welcome the Fear-of-the-Lord.[31] In other words, *"choose this day whom you will serve."*[32]

This experience has caused me to think about how I approach the Lord. I want to approach God with love, my greatest gift of love. I never want to come into His precious presence again in presumption.

How can God be all things at the exact same time? He is the merciful Master while never faltering as the righteous Judge. Our God is essentially happy while also being the Man of Sorrows.[33]

He is for us! His great gift of salvation proves it. As I write this, I pray that this knowledge sinks deeper inside of me. Then when the devil comes to question the goodness of the Lord, I am not shaken, I am not moved, and my love for God is strong enough to lead me, blindly if necessary, closer to the cloud of the Fear-of-the-Lord.

The scriptures say the Lord loved me when I was His enemy.[34] Amazingly, He died for me before I loved Him. With more knowledge, there is a way to love Him more. What was the take-away? Only authentic Fear-of-the-Lord can move me into the very presence of God. It will allow my heart to become cleaner and brighter.[35] It will keep me from presumption. It allows me to come boldly into His presence and ask for the things in accordance with His will. It lets me know His will.

God wants us close!

Who is a God like You, pardoning iniquity and passing over transgression for the remnant of His inheritance? He does not retain His anger forever, because He delights in steadfast love.[36]

NOTES

1. Psalm 16:11
2. John 1:4
3. 2 Corinthians 3:18
4. Psalm 139:13-16
5. John 3:16
6. James 1:17
7. Romans 8:18-22
8. Romans 8:22-24
9. James 4:8
10. Proverbs 9:10
11. Psalm 104:2
12. Daniel 7:9
13. Psalm 139
14. Malachi 3:6
15. Jeremiah 17:9
16. Genesis 3:6-12
17. Genesis 11:1-9
18. Genesis 11:1-9
19. Psalm 24:3-4
20. Jeremiah 17:9
21. Revelation 14:2
22. James 1:20
23. Matthew 7:1
24. Psalm 100:4
25. Proverbs 13:12
26. Isaiah 55:8-9

27. Luke 9:55
28. Exodus 8:19
29. Malachi 1:6
30. Psalm 130:3
31. Proverbs 23:17
32. Joshua 24:15
33. Isaiah 53:3
34. Romans 5:10
35. Psalm 19:9
36. Micah 7:18

CHAPTER 7

✦◆✦

STAINED GARMENT

*"Yes, if you forgive others for the wrongs they do to
you, then your Father in heaven will also forgive your
wrongs. But if you don't forgive others, then your
Father in heaven will not forgive the wrongs you do."*

—MATTHEW 6:14-15 ERV

I also saw a different type of heavenly courtroom.[1] It was a huge room that could hold thousands of people. Think of the size of a coliseum or a stadium. One of the unique abilities of this room was the ability to see and hear as if I was sitting face to face with each person no matter where they were in the room.

I arrived, and although I had never seen anything like this room, I was not in awe. I had a hard heart. Not even being in Heaven could break my hard heart. That should have been the first indicator that I was in great danger. I was filled with a deep-rooted negativity that had turned my heart into a black, hardened disaster. I knew the state of my heart, and I did not care.

I looked in the room, and I was able to see things I couldn't have seen with my earthly eyes. I had been given a pair of heavenly eyes. Heavenly eyes see deeper: they see the motive and love behind every action. With those eyes, I could see the Lord sitting in the center of the room in His cloud of glory.[2] God is *so* much love; He is covered by the cloud.[3] Even with heavenly eyes, I was overwhelmed by Him so I couldn't see all of Him, or I would have been undone.

As I write this, I am again shaken at my stubbornness. That stubbornness that leads to death had taken my heart captive. I sat on a seat made from the glass-like light trees that I had sat on in the previous vision. When I sat, I stopped the outward flow of the light. The light could not pass through me because I was hardhearted. I could see there were three seats made of the same living trees in front of the Lord. Three different people sat on them, and each had black hearts like mine. There were two men and one woman. They were sitting there because they had demanded that the Lord bring His justice to their case. They were not willing to wait for His perfect time. I had arrived in time to watch Him try the cases.

Let me share with you why I had a hard heart that day. Have you ever had something really yucky and ugly happen in your life? Has anyone ever hurt you so much that you thought you may never be able to pick up your life and go on from there? When we get saved, we understand we must forgive, but....

But is a dangerous word when it comes to forgiveness. But what if that wound comes from a fellow believer? A close personal friend, mentor, mother or father in the spirit, sister or brother, pastor, or spouse? Betrayal is a wound that cuts deeply. Betrayal from a believer has the ability to poison another believer very quickly. This had happened in my life and was unresolved.

Knowing that we can deeply wound people, we need to try hard not to hurt one another![4] We should be direct and firm but always keep their hearts in mind. Because we don't have heavenly eyes, we cannot see their heart or the hurt that is already there. We can unknowingly be the fatal blow that causes them to give up in the journey toward their eternal hope of glory. Therefore, we must try to be like Jesus, using love, patience, kindness, forgiveness, and a lot of grace to communicate. To do this well, we need to begin putting on our heavenly eyes. We don't have them now because of sin in our lives. We have to get sin out of our lives so we can see people as Jesus sees them and respond or speak to them as He would.

I didn't always have a hard heart. I was filled with light when I got saved. But someone in the Church really hurt me, and it had reached a boiling point in my life. It had been a long process and we had set yet another meeting. But a solution was not forthcoming. From the previous meetings, the betrayal and misrepresentation now seemed set in stone. I had decided that this would be the last meeting, and I was going to take care of it myself. I felt that the

Matthew 18 approach, a biblical way of handling conflict, had not worked for me. Now it was time to share a juicy tidbit of slander about my accuser. This information would both exonerate me and put that person in their place of being...evil. Why hadn't I brought it sooner? Because this person was a leader.

I have learned much about leadership since that time. No one does it perfectly like Jesus, but we must try. We should never accuse people of being evil. Instead, we should understand that they are sinful like us. We need to watch our tongues![5] What we say about people when we are in conflict with them influences those who are listening. Instead, to be like Jesus as a leader, we need to believe the best about them and for them. Now, I try to be their cheerleader, so that if I need to correct them, they have seen my zeal for them. When I don't understand their actions, I endeavor to believe that they are trying to obey the Lord. I remember that we will spend eternity together, so I treat them like they are the Lord's favorite one, because they are!

I wish I'd had some of that knowledge back then. On the day I was going to take care of this problem myself with my juicy tidbit, the Holy Spirit, thankfully, encountered me before I could murder that leader's reputation.

I went to the restroom to give myself a break from the situation. I looked in the mirror and caught the eye of God. Many times, He corrects me through the mirror. My earthly eye somehow caught His heavenly fiery eyes.

He said, *"You can defend yourself, or I will defend you."*

So I said out loud, *"OK! You defend me, God!"*[6] In my whole-hearted agreement, that tidbit of slander left my memory, never to return.

I walked back into the volatile situation and I had a noticeable peace. I was thinking, *"God is going to strike you all dead."*

Instead, *nothing* happened to show that God was defending me.

I got raked over the coals like you wouldn't believe! It was so hurtful. I left that meeting shocked. God had done nothing to help me. For months, my heart kept yelling at God, *"Where were You?"* To say that I was upset with God was an understatement. I could not understand why He had not defended me. He knew everything, and He let them make me appear guilty when I was innocent.

I was in distress and I knew it was poison. I traveled to see a notable leader in the body of Christ, because I needed wisdom. After I explained everything, including that I forgot my tidbit of slander, he asked me a question: *"Why did God let that happen?"*

My answer was that God did not let it happen. It must have been the devil! The leader explained that it was God in the mirror, and God had let it happen. I insisted that he was wrong. He laughed. I did not appreciate his response at all! He could see my deep distress.

He asked me, *"Laurie, you asked God to let you love like Him?"*

I thought about his question. Yes, I had prayed that over and over. Doesn't everyone?

He went on to explain how Jesus loves the Church who has hurt Him. As His bride I must love His Church like He does. He assured me that God had invited me into a gift but I didn't understand. He shared that letting God defend me is something God assured us is worth whatever the price.

This leader prayed that my heart would see the special offering from God. He also cautioned me to pay close attention, as the gift was not given to the faint of heart. He warned that I must settle my affection because the enemy was looking to devour me.[7]

After I left, my mind constantly repeated the same question. *"Why would God wound me so deeply?"* Over time, my heart began to accuse God, saying, *"He does not care for me."*

Back in the heavenly coliseum, there was a brief break in the glory cloud, and the Lord's fiery eyes met mine. I could see panic in His eyes for me. He felt that I should not be there. At that same moment, the coliseum instantly filled with people, and the glory cloud closed around the Lord in perfection as the Fear-of-the-Lord.

The first case for the woman sitting in front of the Lord was beginning. The people who had filled the coliseum were all those who had participated in her life. There were ones who had cared for her as an infant on the day she was born, teachers, friends, enemies, bus drivers, doctors, co-workers, bosses, neighbors, and acquaintances. Many people had influenced her life, so everyone who had that influence had to come to this court case when she demanded immediate justice.

Even as the trial began, the Lord spoke without words to the angel standing on His left. Without hesitation, the angel stood before me and gripped my arm.

The angel said, *"The Lord wants to meet you in His private chambers. Come with me now!"*

I said, *"No!"* and shook my arm away from his grip.

He had assumed that I would go willingly and quickly with him. But obviously he couldn't tell that I was upset!

The angel regained his grip, now tighter. He repeated himself as if I hadn't heard. My response was the same, but this time louder. The angel was shocked. Oh, the pride of men! Oh, the pride of me! The angel returned to the left side of God and reported my actions.

All of a sudden, the hearing began for the woman. The King spoke, *"If you live in forgiveness, leave now."*

The majority of the room exited. There were hardly any people left with this woman. She was a believer in Jesus Christ. She had been born into a Christian family, attended Christian school, married a Christian man, and her children had accepted the Lord as Savior. She was not able to leave the room because she did not live in forgiveness. Instead, the Lord heard the case, and then He judged rightly.

The real problem with the woman was that she did not trust God. She needed trust in God to be able to forgive others. She did not have the Fear-of-the-Lord in her hard and blackened heart. With much sorrow, the trial ended. Everyone in the room was guilty. The woman and those tied to her life who didn't live in forgiveness were now tied to the guilty sentencing. That is, unless they someday chose to walk in forgiveness in their own lives. If they chose forgiveness, the guilty sentencing would be removed from them. The coliseum emptied because of His judgment, His heart was broken, and these ones were sentenced to hell.

Silence. A frightening lack of any sound brought a sorrowful revelation to those in the courtroom who had ears to hear.

Seeing and hearing should have caused the two waiting men to forgive. However, because of their hard hearts, they didn't forgive.[8] The Lord can *fix* every wrong thing *if* we live by His Fear-of-the-Lord.

The angel came again quickly to me and said, *"The Lord would rather meet you in His private chambers...please!"*

I suddenly realized that I was in more danger than I comprehended. If my life had been tied in any way to those men, I would have been in danger of being sentenced to hell, like the others. I might have become like Pharaoh in the Bible who was so hardhearted that no correction could penetrate him, even to save him.[9]

The angel whisked me into the Lord's private chambers.

As I entered, I noticed the Lord was extremely serious. The panic I had seen in His eyes was still there. I also understood that He held His deep concern for my life in perfect check. He wouldn't remove my free choice.

He said, *"Laurie Ann, you cannot be in that courtroom with your heart!"*

I understood that my life was in imminent danger. I wanted—no, needed—to explain. Even as I formed the thoughts to share, I knew that I was wrong. I just couldn't tell why I was wrong.

I answered, *"Lord, You said You would defend me."*

He was firm while being patient. He said, *"The time hasn't come yet."*

I continued in my limited understanding, *"No, no, Lord, the time is past."*

Unbelievably, in His presence, the rest of the pain and accusation toward God continued to pour out of my dark and hard heart. I told Him how the leaders had misrepresented me. I shared with Him the name I had been called—Jezebel. I told Him how the weight was too much for me. The Bible records the Lord as saying that she, Jezebel, should not be tolerated![10] I wept bitterly from the wounds that were inflicted from the Church. I felt rejected by them and by Him.

All the pain and anger rose out of the deepest part of my heart. Then I reminded Him that He had said He would defend me, but instead He had thrown me under the bus.[11] I had no control to stop the words. He was in control, demanding that the accusations in my hard heart release me. I was only sharing things that were embedded in my heart, as if together we were performing surgery.

When I was finished spilling all the blackness out of my heart, I bowed my head. I noticed the material of the stunningly white robe He wore. It was a garment that only He could wear, perfect and created for the purpose to judge.[12] It covered His body in a light that had been established from truth that is from the beginning of time, the foundation of times. This garment was proof that only He can render righteous judgment. Hallelujah!

As I studied the material, it caused a desire for this truth to defend me. My desire for truth was needed in my will. Before, I only wanted *my way*, which meant that I was dealing in manipulation, working against the will of Jesus. I felt His anger leave, now replaced with relief. He would not take away my ability to choose, but now my choice was aligned with truth—with Him.[13]

I felt the atmosphere change. I looked up into His eyes. He was blinding in His brilliance.[14] He had to turn down His brightness so that I could see Him. I knew He was staring intently at me. I remembered many of the mighty things He had done for me in my past. It came to me from somewhere deep inside, almost as if I had a default chip placed inside of me from when I was created, like a back door into a security system that the Creator placed there to always have access. I knew I shouldn't look away.[15] Instead, I submitted to the simple choice—look deeper. His eyes held the fire that could burn away all the hardness that had stopped my heart from being like His.

I had great pain inside me from others. I felt that the arrows they had shot were a direct hit to my heart, where they had exploded and destroyed my identity. I didn't think I had a heart anymore.

He saw my pain, my submission, and my lack of knowledge.

He said: *"Come here, child."*

The word "come" has such a healing effect. Immediately tears streamed out of my eyes.[16] With each tear, my heart was being released. He held me and wrapped me in the garment of truth. I sobbed uncontrollably. When my tears subsided, I stepped back, concerned that I had left tear stains on His garment. Tears did not affect the garment.

Wrapped in His truth, I understood why He had been so upset to see me so hard-hearted in His courtroom. I was guilty with unforgiveness, and had my life touched those men, I too would be so hard, like Pharaoh, that I would have been forever lost and eternally separated from Him.[17] Thank God that He saw me sitting there. I am so thankful that He sent His angel to warn me!

The Lord had a plan. He took the sleeve of His amazing robe, and He tucked it so that He had something to wipe the shame and pain and all the messy makeup from my face. As He wiped all of my face, these things smeared a mess into the sleeve of the garment.

I saw it and was upset. It was ruined. How could He wear this now? I had wrecked His perfect garment. He actually thought my worries about His garment were humorous. I was worried about His robe instead of being worried about my soul. Tears do not affect the garment unless the wearer is affected.

He showed me the messy sleeve and said, *"Do you see this mark? I won't forget what has happened to you. I've collected all the tears and all the pain.*[18] *I won't forget!"*

I understood that the only way the stain would leave the robe would be when the people who hurt me ask Him for forgiveness of their sins. Who is this God who would carry my tear stains as a reminder of what had happened to me?

I was trying to understand. He made a statement that I knew required my agreement.

"Trust me?"

That was the whole problem—the problem that caused the terrible fall in the garden and the problem that was causing my heart to be susceptible to the hardness. I needed to trust that in the *right time*, He would defend me. I had proof, the mark on His beautiful garment. In His presence, I understood that the battle was not finished. Every day I need to guard against an attack about His goodness. I knew I was healed. My heart was alive and filled with compassion.

He returned to the courtroom to listen to the cases of the two men waiting. I hoped they were already gone because the outcome would not be good.

"How can I keep this truth?" I asked as He was leaving.

He turned and walked over to me. He placed His hands on either side of my face. He looked in my being, through my eyes, and spoke one word.

"Remember."[19]

That word was filled with the Fear-of-the-Lord. I needed to remember who He is, what He has done, how He has proven Himself, and believe that He will do everything according to His perfect plan. His timing will be *perfect!*[20]

"Forgive me, Lord!" were the words coming out of me as I returned.

I had received a new understanding. Satan has used people to hurt my life, and he has used me to hurt others. No matter the accusation I have against someone, I am guilty of the same thing. Only Jesus can fix all the wrongs. There is a place to meet the Lord—at the Cross, through the act of taking communion. As we partake, we remember who He is and what He did on the Cross when He spilled His blood for us. This tenderizes our hearts and wraps them in a protective barrier, insulated against unforgiveness and hardness of heart—until the next offense comes along.

The only way to succeed is to become unoffendable by completely submitting ourselves to the perfect ways of Jesus. Anything less leaves us in danger of being tied to someone whose case is being heard or, even worse, being the one to demand justice in His courtroom.

NOTES

1. Daniel 7:9-10
2. 2 Chronicles 5:14
3. Exodus 40:34
4. Matthew 7:12
5. Proverbs 12:18, Proverbs 18:21
6. Isaiah 51:22
7. 1 Peter 5:8
8. Mark 3:5
9. Exodus 9:12
10. Revelation 2:20
11. Psalm 145:18
12. Psalm 104:2
13. John 8:32
14. Revelation 1:16
15. Job 7:19
16. Jeremiah 31:9

17. Exodus 8:15
18. Psalm 56:8
19. James 1:22-25
20. 2 Peter 3:8-9, Ecclesiastes 3:1-13

CHAPTER 8

---◆◆◆---

SUMMONED CELEBRATION

"This I recall to my mind, therefore I have hope.
*Through the **Lord's** mercies we are not consumed,*
because His compassions fail not. They are new
*every morning; great is **Your** faithfulness."*

—LAMENTATIONS 3:21-24

I'd like to tell you about one of the times that I danced with Jesus. I was at a very special party with all of Heaven in attendance. In this vision, I was with my husband, Mike. I also saw our oldest daughter there with her husband.

Later, it seemed confusing to see them there while we are all still alive. Holy Spirit helped me understand by reminding me that the Bible says, *"We are seated in heavenly places with the Lord."*[1] I believe we are all a part of Heaven while still on the earth. If we can grasp the principles of Heaven, we can have God's will here on earth the way it is in Heaven just like it says in the Bible, *"Thy Kingdom come, Thy will be done on earth as it is in Heaven."*[2]

The first thing I knew in the vision was that I was in a fantastic and mystical place, inside the mystery of God. I am going to call these unexplainable things "mystical" in an attempt to explain the unexplainable. I was surrounded by a tunnel made of living stones, and as I ran my hand along them, they encouraged me by their love for God. Their love increased mine. I have since held earthly rocks to see if I can feel the same connection, but I do not.

Everything in Heaven sparkles like prisms of cut glass. It has a very supernatural effect because the majority of glass we know is thick and plain. The glass in Heaven sparkles like the blinding brilliance of the sun dancing on the waves of Lake Superior and the sun shining through icy covered branches after an ice storm. Many things are made out of glass in Heaven, and it is an architectural miracle how these things stay put. Once I saw these *huge* glass doors that were at least three stories tall and maybe three feet deep. They had small glass hinges holding them in place. As I looked at the way they were built, it reaffirmed the amazing abilities of our Creator God. I kept looking at the doors. Jesus laughed that I was so excited about glass.

He teasingly said, *"It's just dirt."*

But His most prized creation, also made of mere dirt, is mankind.[3] Being impressed that He heated sand to make glass is nothing compared to the majesty of using dust to create man in His own image. I look at people so much differently now. Can you see the *image of God!*[4] Everyone is extra special!

The castle rocks all sparkled like this heavenly glass. Somehow by touching them, they implanted their love sparkle inside of me. I don't know how that happens, but everything in Heaven is connected.[5] If you are a Kingdom citizen, then right now as you read this you are connected to Heaven itself. We fit, and we belong! Everything works with a wonderful connecting purpose if we join it.

Embedded in the stone wall were amazing white fire lights like sconces all along the corridor. These flames never went out. They were alive and, like the life-giving breath of God, had their origin from our God who is an all-consuming fire.[6]

On earth, we have fire that is red, orange, yellow, and even a blue, but our fire has no emotion. The fire along the stone tunnel was filled with happy emotion when I touched it.

I reached up to touch the white fire light, which radiated through my whole arm but did not burn me. Instead, it felt like warm oil and left me with that goosebumps feeling you get when touched by someone who loves you.

Although I was in a hurry, I would have loved to place my whole being inside one of those flames. I believe it must be similar to the fire that Shadrach, Meshach, and Abednego stood inside.[7]

I was on a stone stairway that was held together by the spoken word of the Lord.[8] The way the stairway was constructed, it could not stand architecturally on its own. It was the command of God that anchored it. Under His direction, the stairway would always be perfectly safe. As I was moving up the stairway, I knew that the whole tunnel was moving. I couldn't wait to see where it was taking me. There are many things in Heaven that work very differently than here on earth. The stairway is only one.

In this vision, I was going to an event. To try and explain this mystical gathering, I will call it a "summoned celebration." The Lord summoned us all because He wanted to celebrate with everyone. I knew in my heart it was an honor to be able to hear His voice call me and to come. He only called out one word from His heart, *"Come!"* When His word reached me, I was filled with love, appreciation, acceptance, honor, strength, identity, desire, passion, and on and on. Somehow, like everyone else, I was on my way.

The Bible tells of a time when Peter saw the Lord walking on the water and wanted to join Him. Peter called out and asked to join Him. Jesus said, *"Come!"* Then, Peter walked on the water too.[9] We can do amazing things in God when we hear His voice bid us, *"Come!"*

I was wearing a very beautiful dress, as were all the ladies. Everyone's clothing was made of the same material in a time period that they chose. My dress had an empire waist and was extra detailed because of the importance of the celebration. I've worn a lot of empire waist dresses in Heaven because they are always very modest and beautiful. Actually, that style is very popular in Heaven and stunning on everyone who chooses it.

By putting on a heavenly made dress, somehow, every girl embraces and enjoys their femininity and is a "girly girl" in Heaven.

All the girls are happy and comfortable being made female. God's idea of what it means to be female is more girly than I expected. In Heaven, all women fit perfectly in their femininity.[10]

The material of our clothing was something mystical. It was similar to sequins but so much more. Somehow it worked together with me to be whatever color I desired. That is, until it was in the presence of love, which caused it to radiate white light. Many people standing together radiated the mystical white light with stunning brilliance.

Mike and I were laughing as we ran with many other people up the stone staircase. It curved onto the floor where the celebration was being held. I was so excited to be a part of the "important" people at this event. Everyone is important, but it felt wonderful to know that I am important to Him too. There were important people both in front of and behind us. Everyone knew the importance of the people next to him or her.

All of us were hurrying to be with God. In Heaven, we never had to worry about falling down and breaking anything. People can fall down, but they don't get hurt. Sometimes the falling down is just as much fun as running. It is like being dropped as a child onto the top of a bed. It tickles your tummy.

I was running up the wide stairs using my legs, but the people who live in Heaven could fly. I say "fly," but it was more like float-moving. I couldn't fly yet. Instead the rocks and the stairs helped move me by pushing me up as I ran. There was no need of escalators or elevators because the stairs happily helped those with less-than-heavenly bodies to not grow weary by doing the work for us.

When I reached the top of the staircase, I looked across the wide-open space of the room we had entered and realized that I was standing in outer space. It was remarkable! I stepped onto a large, stunning platform. It was made of some sort of see-through glass. I could see the stars below the glass, above me and around me. I was standing in space. There were no walls, just the floor created from God's command and placed somewhere in the galaxy, surrounded by stars that were already dancing for the Lord.

It was breathtaking. A supernatural excitement, that I cannot adequately explain, filled me as I reveled in being in the galaxy for a party that the Lord had summoned me to attend. *Who* can hold such a party? Only Jesus!

I looked across from my spiral stone staircase to another large spiral staircase bringing people down onto the glass floor. They too were running and experiencing great pleasure. I was in awe. It wasn't due to the multitude of people, although that was very impressive, but it was because of the stairwell. There was no way that staircase could be hanging out in space the way it was.

As I watched the people running down, I saw my daughter with her husband join the celebration. I was so very happy to see them! She had chosen a different style of dress. It was all lace and had a big poof at her waist sticking out maybe a distance of three feet. I was shocked to see her in that style, as she would never have chosen it on earth. It was much too girly for her. At the ball, she was stunning, and she could not have chosen a better dress. Her husband chose a short waist jacket with a wide cummerbund and knickers with stockings. *What?* He would never choose this style on earth, but in Heaven he understood his importance and the importance of being summoned by the *King*. So he *dressed up!* He looked absolutely amazing!

I believe a lot of people are going to Heaven, many whom I may not have seen at the summoned celebration. But I am thankful the Lord chose to allow me to see my daughter and son-in-law who will live eternally in Heaven someday. It was glorious to know that those who have "ears to hear God" will be there.[11]

Our kids were with an entirely different group of people than Mike and I. There was no need to try to reposition myself as I was right where I needed to be. I looked again at the stairway, and it was moving across the galaxy placing excited people onto the glass dance floor. *How?* Creator God is not limited to my understanding. ☺

I was deposited from the stairway in the location of the dancing group the Lord had prepared for me. Everyone was in groups, dancing in circles. It was a big party dancing with the stars. The dance itself was similar to square dancing style. I did square dancing in elementary school so I understand the concept of group dancing. This was, however, some sort of wonderful Jewish dancing that I have never known. Mike and I are not coordinated to dance fancy, but there were no issues in Heaven.

When I looked down through the glass floor, I saw the stars lighting up a pathway to help me know where to step. They were helping people like us so that we could fit right in. A nice, refreshing wind was blowing through. I thought to myself that I didn't know there was wind in the galaxy. Mike laughed as he heard my thoughts and so did everyone else.

"When did I ever dance in the galaxy to know there was wind?" We all laughed and kept on dancing.

We moved around inside of our dancing group. I always liked when I made it back to Mike. In my life, Mike has shared with me so many God stories and experiences that being there with him made my heart extra happy. The old and the young, everyone was clapping and dancing. Each circle was having so much fun.

The music we danced to came from the stars—their noise filled the galaxy! And the moves of the heavenly dance caused us to reach out and link hands to wrists as we spun and twirled. I was dancing with different people, weaving in and out, grabbing different people's hands. Then, all of a sudden, as we were finally working in unison, the Lord appeared on the glass floor inside of our group.

We understood that He enters each circle eventually. As far as we could see, people were dancing. The dancing went on and on and on because the Lord was going from this circle to that circle. He would dance in every circle. That was really exciting. There was also no impatience, as we knew He would come when the time was right, and until then we kept having fun. It didn't matter that He wasn't in our circle. We weren't really paying attention to what was happening in other circles because we had the knowledge that He would come to ours.

As we were weaving in and out, reaching for a new hand, there He was. All of a sudden, it was my turn. He slapped His arm against mine and took me out of the circle. He smiled at me, and I heard Him in my heart say my name. I love when Jesus says my name. When He says it, I know that all is right. He said something else that was like a command for every part of my being. As He spoke, my whole spirit rejoiced!

"REMEMBER, I LOVE YOU!"

We continued doing this same unique twirl as on the glass floor, but now we were out in the universe where there was no glass floor. Oh, my goodness!

The stars were passing through us, and they were tickling me everywhere. It was so mystical! The Lord twirled me around. He wanted to show me what He had made out in the galaxy. I thought things like, "How do the stars pass through me, and where do I put my feet to dance?" But suddenly I realized, "It's alright, I am with Jesus, and He can take me anywhere!" I was safer with Him than on the glass floor.

He'll take us everywhere and show us everything that He's made if we are willing to go with Him. But it takes trust.[12] I knew in my heart, I trusted the Lord, and I would never stop! Once He knew that I felt safe with Him, He began twirling me around at such a rate, racing me across the galaxy. He showed me remarkable things! At the same time, while seeing absolutely breathtaking sights, I understood that I am still His highest creation. *Wow!* He had summoned me to give me wisdom and revelation as to my importance. He summoned the whole celebration to make a memory for and with each of us.

I saw the sun and the moon and other suns and mountains made up of mystical galaxy material. I saw designs and plans and areas that looked like waterfalls made out of special universe lights. We looked at a black hole, and when He turned it I saw it was the bottom of a type of mystical hourglass. With each stunning creation, I knew that the Creator was sharing His life with me, like in the way that I share my God moments with Mike. Only now, my highest desire was to share each moment with Christ.

Although overwhelmed by His love, my physical body was spent. It was emotionally exhausting in a wonderful way to realize my importance to Him! Even though He had shown me amazing things, all I wanted to do now was look at Him.[13] He is the *Almighty!* He is the one who loves me more than I will ever comprehend. He is amazing and worthy of complete adoration. He is and will forever be altogether lovely![14]

He understood my desire to freeze time and let it all become a memory I would never forget. He gave me a gift of remembrance and allowed it to be a statue in my garden.

He spoke to my spirit again, *"Remember, I love you!"*[15]

He looked at me, and I knew things about my identity that I might not have been able to comprehend had I not attended the dance. He shared from His heart the fun He had showing me His creation and letting all those stars tickle us. His eyes never left mine as He danced me back around. Suddenly His feet hit the floor first, and then He helped me get my balance on the glass before He let me go. He handed me to another dancer in our circle, and I was filled with greater joy than I have words to explain.

Next, He grabbed Mike. The Lord didn't miss a beat. His energy is limitless. He was ready for His dance with Mike. I know on the earth some people say they don't believe in dancing. Well, Jesus believes in dancing! As the Lord grabbed Mike, I yelled to him, *"Mike, you are going to love it!"*

In a flash, Mike was away with the Lord! I knew he would be forever changed by this summoned celebration, but especially because of the dance. As the Lord took Mike away, the dancing on the glass floor didn't stop, and neither did the love or the closeness between us. In fact, as each person returned from being with Jesus, the celebration became, more and more, the most important day ever lived. Collectively, we shone brighter because of the knowledge of who we are.

I came out of the vision slowly. I knew I had left the dance, but I lingered in the love of my friends, especially that of Jesus. I kept my eyes shut knowing that someday I would be there forever. I sealed the memory with His words, *"Remember, I love you!"*

Jesus gave me this remarkable memory because memories help us to hold fast to an untold future. Memories can help us trust, have faith, and not quit. Memories are like the stars under the glass. A memory can light the way back to the right pattern of happiness. They show us how to get through the problem. Memories of my time with Jesus are like the fire on the walls in Heaven that light up and make us feel that lovely, goosebumpy happiness.

Making memories in Heaven is important to Jesus! Making memories that tie us to Jesus is important on earth too. Memories of God and His goodness help us through hard places until we can spend eternity with Him. It's really fun to be with people we love, especially when we can do something extra special with them. These memories are important in good times, but more important in bad times. Being together can be mystical if we let it. Someday we will all be together. We must keep this in mind when we feel alone, afraid, sick, and hurting.

My time in Heaven helps me remember the mystical truths that Jesus showed me, and they strengthen me to face the hard times up ahead in my life on earth.

I must remember that I am loved![16]

When it is hard, really hard in this life, I have to choose to remember. I change my state of mind so that the momentary light afflictions don't cause me to give up and give in to the lies of the enemy.[17] Moving from a place of pain isn't easy, but it is doable. I came back knowing this—knowing that no matter what, I am loved, and at the right time I will be in Heaven.

The scriptures say, *"Thy kingdom come, Thy will be done on earth as it is in Heaven."*[18] If we knew how it worked in Heaven, then we could do it here on the earth. We spend too much energy thinking about pain and suffering and entertaining the destructive thoughts that go through us. Put something in place to cover those bad times in your life. The Bible teaches us to *"Think on things above."*[19] Therefore, we must change our focus to our eternal destiny.[20]

I had to figure out what to do with all the pain locked inside because of my grandbaby's death. We lost this little one due to a miscarriage not long ago. Our daughter was in the hospital nearly losing her life too. It was a very hard time for our family! I yearned for a happy memory here on earth to tie something good to that heart-wrenching loss. I knew this would help me reach Jesus and show the rest of my family the way. In my pain, the Holy Spirit brought the memory of what it was like to dance with Jesus in the stars. We decided to hold a summoned family gathering to celebrate the one who now lives in Heaven as our Practically Perfect Person. I cried out in my heart to Jesus, *"Come!"*

An idea came to me. I bought everyone a can of silly string, and we had a silly string war. The kids thought it was great to spray their parents. The grown-ups soon began participating, and in no time we were all laughing and feeling loved. Nothing will stop the ache of missing our little one who resides with Jesus. There are no answers to the many questions. Instead, we are a people who will remember our great God and make a memory to shut the door on the enemy who is hoping to heap infection into a wound that may not heal this side of Heaven. God uses memories to begin healing our pain. He promises to give us joy for our ashes. That's our strength.

> *But the Helper, the Holy Spirit, whom the Father will send in My name, He will teach you all things, **and bring to your remembrance all things that I said to you.***[21]

NOTES

1. Ephesians 2:6
2. Matthew 6:10
3. Genesis 2:7
4. Genesis 1:27, James 3:9
5. Romans 8:28
6. Hebrews 12:29
7. Daniel 3:25
8. Hebrews 1:3, Colossians 1:17
9. Matthew 14:29
10. Genesis 5:2
11. Revelation 2:29, Matthew 11:15
12. Proverbs 3:5-6
13. Exodus 34:35
14. Song of Solomon 4:7, Song of Solomon 5:16
15. 1 John 4:7-21
16. John 3:16
17. 2 Corinthians 4:17, Romans 8:18
18. Matthew 6:10
19. Colossians 3:1
20. Philippians 4:8
21. John 14:26

CHAPTER 9

THE THIMBLE CUP

"I have given you authority to trample on snakes
and scorpions and to overcome all the power
of the enemy; nothing will harm you."

—LUKE 10:19 NIV

During the 2020 COVID-19 pandemic, we lived under stay-at-home orders across the country to help stop the spread of the virus. There was much fear all around, especially for those with a compromised immune system. At that time, my immune system was at risk so I was very concerned. In the midst of this, I had an encounter where the Lord showed me how I should respond. The timing, during the writing of this book, was perfect. The Lord used the encounter to help me understand an issue of authority that needs to be addressed.

Like everyone, I was at home. I was being extra cautious for a number of real reasons. People were not sure about the virus, how it transferred, how long it stayed on surfaces, or how to survive it. I wore a mask when I went out, just in case I had it inside of me. I did not want to pass it along to someone who had a compromised immune system, nor did I want to get it and pass it along inside of my family. However, I am an evangelist, and the best time to share the gospel is in a crisis.

So I would go to the grocery store and ask various elderly people how I might help them. They were very stressed because panic filled the atmosphere. After I helped them and we loaded their groceries into the car, I would ask them about Jesus, if I hadn't already.[1] I had *many* wonderful conversations. Many people already knew Jesus but needed to reconnect. They were very glad that He had sent me. Some people did not know God personally. To them I gave literature that I keep on hand, as well as my book, *The Hell Conspiracy*.

During that time, I asked God in my prayers if He would show me what else to do. Until then, I would continue what I was doing. His answer didn't come right away, but I am sure it came right on time.

As the encounter began, I was bowing low and gazing at an incredible floor unlike anything I had ever seen. It was very smooth, even slippery, like glass and extremely difficult to stand on.[2] It had lightning inside of it.[3] The lightning was sent across the floor, and when it reached me, it exploded and deposited inside of me a power to accomplish something specific. There was also an intense wind in the room that was blowing hard in all directions.

The wind directed and began moving me backward toward a doorway. I was not moving quickly because of the amount of lightning being sent across the floor to equip me. I hadn't looked at the person who was sending the lightning because I was completely overwhelmed from what I had seen when I had last looked up. Everything is in the Lord's mighty command, as was the wind and the lightning.[4] He was creating a storm that moved through the conduit of the remarkable floor.

I thought the lightning was going to kill me. I could see it explode all around me through the floor. I was the lightning rod, and each intensified bolt found me. I noticed from my peripheral vision that a huge door to my right had opened. Even though I was bowing low, the wind would pick me up as soon as the floor had delivered the power from the lightning bolt. I was sure that these walls could not contain the blast of that wind.

The last bolt hit me so hard that it popped me straight up, and then an even more intense blast of wind pushed me through the threshold of the door. Once I cleared the doorway, huge white doors made of a fog closed, and I was able to stand up fully.

Instead of feeling spent, I felt exhilarated!

I looked around very excited and met the eyes of my angel. This angel had been assigned to me when I entered the room and knew everything that I had just experienced. I looked up at him and was speechless!

I had so much excitement trapped inside of me that I did the only thing I could think to do and began running. As I ran, he chased me—not to catch me but to train me. I looked back and so much joy seemed to explode out of me.[5] I was breathless, and yet somehow the act of becoming breathless increased my energy to run.

I was running down a magnificent corridor filled with doors. Each door was an entry point into the corridor. Other angels could enter this hallway from wherever they had been assigned. It was wide, white, endless, and filled with anticipation. My angel must have entered through one of these doorways. But all of that was irrelevant now as we had both been assigned to do something for the King.

As I ran, this angel coached me. He would come close and cause more of the joy inside of me to explode. As it did, a squeal of pure joy escaped my lungs, much the way a small child screams when a parent chases them.

Too soon I reached what appeared to be the end of the corridor. As I began to slow down, the angel sped up, and his authority opened the end of the corridor to show me that there was yet another seemingly endless pathway. I understood that I should run. Run fast, run far, run and do not stop.

The angel would purposely come close, almost catching me, to cause the breathlessness to refuel me. I was in great delight! Why is breathlessness so important? Because when we have emptied ourselves, we can tap into His strength. In our weakness, He is strong.[6]

Finally, we reached an elevator. There was no button to call for the elevator. Even if there had been, I had no authority to call it to come. As I waited the split second for the angel to arrive behind me, I could see how much he loved the run too. In my breathless laughter, I choked out how I hadn't had this much fun since kindergarten, to which he nodded approvingly.

Then I realized that I had just left the Throne Room of God and the lightning had come directly from the King. I was different—on purpose and for a purpose. I had been commissioned by God.

When the angel arrived, the elevator doors opened. We entered, and I began chatting with him. As the elevator moved, I told him what a great runner I am. He laughed and agreed. I wasn't saying that I was fast or better than anyone, just that I was great. I was great because I ran very far, I didn't quit, and I finished without getting distracted.[7] These were the qualifiers that made it true to claim that I was a great runner. In all my excitement, I continued talking non-stop.

I asked him, *"Do you think I can do it?"*

Before he could answer, I asked another *question "Do you think they will believe me?"*

He gave me a quick smile and shrugged his shoulders as if to say he didn't know.

I declared, *"I am a very good storyteller!"*

To which he answered, *"Yes, you are!"*

Then I told him, *"I get it from my grandfather who was a great storyteller!"*

The angel answered, *"Yes, he is!"*

Abruptly, the elevator doors opened, and I was now supposed to take the message that I had been given to the Church.

I suddenly got worried. I asked the angel again if he thought they would believe me.

He said, *"You were not asked to get them to believe you, only to tell them!"*[8]

I understood. I asked the angel if I could practice what I was going to say with him. He agreed.

I began, *"When you first got saved..."*

The angel interrupted to say, *"I have always been saved."* I smiled at him and asked again if I could *practice* what I was going to say. He agreed.

I restarted, *"When you first got saved, you were given a little cup like this one."* I showed him my thimble.

I continued, *"And inside of here is more than enough of the blood of Jesus to take care of all of our problems."*[9]

As I stuck my finger inside the container, there was one drop of blood that looked like water.

I continued, *"You must apply the blood of Jesus to the issue, and it is His authority that will make it all happen."*[10]

Then I demonstrated for the angel. I put the blood across my chest.

I continued to tell him, *"It doesn't matter what the problem is because there is no problem that can stand up to Jesus and the mark of His blood."*[11] I then mentioned several problems to him, including the virus.

I explained that if the virus is the problem, then stick your finger in and take the one drop to put on it. Put one drop on any sickness, and it has to submit. I explained how the drop would look like water, and it is only activated by faith.[12] But with faith, that drop of blood could do anything.[13]

I shared how I do not have all authority. Jesus does. It is OK if my authority does not change something; I am just a woman. When Jesus sends His authority, every door will open, every problem will cease, and the thimble will *never* run out.

The angel told me, *"You have it exactly right!"*

Then without words I understood that I needed to run with this truth. Run to tell the Church who has forgotten about applying the blood of Jesus. The Church needed to remember and I needed to run just like when I left the Throne Room. I needed to run the way I ran down the halls with the angel chasing me—with joy and wonder. I needed to run and become breathless. When we are breathless, we have given all of our strength and are made weak so then the Lord can give us His strength.[14]

I knew I couldn't just tell a few, but I had to *run* to tell everyone.[15] I had to keep running and not quit. I had to finish without getting distracted. As I had run in that hallway, I was being trained how to run with endurance.[16] I would get tired and think, *It doesn't matter anyway because the angel is going to catch me,* and I would almost give up. Then angel would reenergize me as he continued the chase.

I cannot stop, slow down, give up, or think about who is behind me. I cannot look to the right or the left. I must finish.

The angel said, *"Yes, perfect!!"*

He told me not to stop, no matter what. He assured me that just like my training in the corridor, he would be there chasing me. Who knew that had been my training? But because I was fully equipped, I did not have an excuse not to accomplish the task. He explained that this time I would not see him chasing me. I understood that I do not have all authority; God does. And He had sent the angel to go with me to open the doors that I could not.

I exited the elevator and took another look at him. He was right; I was not commissioned to get people to believe me but only to tell them. Of course I could do it, I just needed to begin by becoming breathless.

As I began to run, I saw many church people everywhere—pastors, teachers, evangelists, prophets, and apostles. They all needed to know or at least be reminded that they too have a thimble of the blood of Jesus. I turned around, and I could see the angel as he slowly became invisible. I knew he would be chasing along with me. I also was reminded from my training that I should enjoy this task, and at that I let out a squeal.[17]

When the encounter ended, I was still filled with the zeal to run and tell everyone.[18] Jesus has given us all we need to succeed! The reality is that I do not have all authority, but I know the One who does.[19] Applying the blood of Jesus to the situations that need help is our act of faith. I was able to apply this immediately to the question that had worried me, "Do I have COVID?" I realized that even if I did, it had no authority over me because the blood in the cup was stronger.

Jesus will send the needed guidance and help necessary for all of us to accomplish the task He has commissioned us to do.[20] However, if we don't run with the same fervor I learned in the hallway, we won't know where to begin.[21] If we are looking at a problem and don't have an outcome in mind, we won't know how to run or we will stop before we've won. We must run until we become breathless and let His strength carry us. We must run, not stopping to worry about what we can't do because we can do all things through Christ who strengthens us![22]

Our faith is the gunshot that says run. And then we run.

Notes

1. 2 Timothy 4:2
2. Revelation 4:6
3. Revelation 4:5
4. Matthew 8:27
5. 1 Peter 1:8
6. 2 Corinthians 12:10, Isaiah 40:31
7. 2 Timothy 4:7-9
8. 1 Corinthians 3:5-9, Ezekiel 2:7
9. Colossians 1:20
10. Hebrews 10:19
11. Revelation 12:11
12. Hebrews 11:6
13. Mark 9:23

14. 2 Corinthians 13:9
15. Mark 16:15
16. Hebrews 12:1
17. John 15:11
18. 1 Peter 1:2
19. Matthew 28:18-20
20. Philippians 4:13
21. Hebrews 12:1-2
22. Philippians 4:13, John 14:12

CHAPTER 10

---◆◆---

THE HARD WAY

*"But small is the gate and narrow the road
that leads to life, and only a few find it."*

—MATTHEW 7:14 NIV

My favorite pastime is to daydream about when I will live in Heaven forever. It makes me very happy and sometimes quite homesick. Things are very different there. I will be very different there. For instance, I will not want so much independence. What I want when I am in Heaven is to be *with* the Lord.[1]

Jesus can come get you whenever He wants to if you trust Him and give Him permission to make your life what He desires it to be. One of my favorite and most frequent prayers is: *"I want to come be with You, Jesus!"* I believe it makes Him happy to know that He matters so much to me. I want to be with Jesus wherever He is, all the time.

You know the prayer taught to little children to pray before bed: *"Now I lay me down to sleep, I pray the Lord my soul to keep. If I should die before I wake, I pray the Lord my soul to take."*

I think that prayer is scary. I never liked repeating it. Who wants to think about dying as they are shutting their eyes? Now I know I will never die. Instead, I like to tell children, *"Ask God to catch you just before you fall asleep and take you on the best adventures ever."* Some children have shared that He took them to see Noah building the ark and they were able to pet all the animals. Others have played ball or had a tea party with Him. I ask God to just come get me no matter what He is doing. I find myself pleading before I go to sleep that I just want to come to be with Him. Many times, He does take me away with Him. I am sure that He thinks of my pestering Him as endearing.

Everybody has a special place to live that is prepared by Jesus. He will come to visit all His loved ones at each and every house. The Lord also lives in a house with many rooms, and some people will live in His big house with Him.[2] These are the ones who get to hang out with Him more than anyone else. I want to live in His house. To me, Heaven's best reward is to be one of the people who are closest to Him. There are a great number of people who live with Him. I need to be one of those people. I don't want to have my own house where He can come visit me just every once in a while. Instead, I want to live in community with Him and all the people who need to be close to Him. That "needing Him" started when I got saved. It is a treasure that keeps me close.

I realize if I tell these things about Heaven then the crowd that wants to live at His house will get bigger. His house is *huge* and living together with you there will be wonderful! In fact, I hope that I have caused you to desire it with your whole being. Otherwise, I would not be worthy to be one chosen to live there.

Heaven is a Kingdom that doesn't exploit needing one another. Instead, it thrives on it. I understood this principle when meeting Jesus the first time, and I have clung to it. I know who He is—Friend, King, Savior, Lord, Brother, and the list goes on and on. I know where He is—patiently waiting in Heaven until our Father tells Him to come for us. I can't wait until we can all be together forever! For now, I try to help as many people as possible meet Jesus so that they may spend eternity with Him.[3]

Once I get there, I don't want to be separated from Him ever again. I want to be with that group of people who hang out with Him every single day. Whether I'm the one who goes and gets Him a drink of water or sharpens His pencil, I don't care! I want to be in that large group of people who hang out with Jesus *every day*.

And then there is another, even more exclusive group. It is those who travel with Jesus. I hope I am counted worthy to be a part of this exclusive group. Wherever He goes, from house to house to house, this select group of people goes with Him. I want to be with these wonderful people who accompany Jesus when He goes to all of the other houses. How do we end up in that group?

Our obedience on the earth determines many things in Heaven. It increases the glory we will have there.

Once, in a vision, I went to a room in Heaven like no other. I will call it the Strategy Room. The timing of the vision was amazing. I am sure I will never forget it! I was driving down a two-lane highway going 55 miles per hour. I was singing along with a Christian CD and all of a sudden, *bam!* I'm in Heaven.

When I arrived in the heavenly Strategy Room, an angel held my arm. It was firm and helpful. The angel had his wings on, so I knew it was official business. When the angel released me, I was a little off balance so he stood behind me with his hands on both of my elbows to steady me.

The Lord was in front of me looking at a table directly in front of Him. The table was very unique. It came up from a pedestal and was big enough to hold everything that would be placed on it, no matter how big. It was also a calculating table. I knew that it could weigh things like a scale at the grocery store.

The table was describing my life to Jesus, and it could also identify the lies in my life. It could also dial in like a microscope so that nothing was hidden about my life.

We don't have anything like this here. I'm going to try to explain it because your life will be analyzed on this table as well. There were sections of one's life that Jesus could add or take off depending on His will. The table easily balanced itself to all changes. As I looked at the table from a bird's-eye view, I could see the earth through the table. It was beautiful with mountains and water, and miraculously everything stayed inside the edge of this table. Layers were added depending on the day or days the Lord was reviewing.

As I arrived, Jesus commanded time to enter the table. This is going to sound crazy; there is nothing that I have in my vocabulary to explain sufficiently, but I will try. Time, as we know it, was like a cylinder of moving light. It stood in the room, and everyone could see it. Jesus wanted my "times" to come out of the cylinder and join the table.[4] Time came out of the container in a large round shape, much like a huge pizza. It moved and laid itself on top of the table, and the square shape of the table changed to a circle.

I struggle to find words about how this all occurred. The first "pizza" was of my past. It began right from the minute I was conceived. It settled into the table, and it took a form like concrete. These things were hardened because of the length of time that had passed.

Next, another disk came out of the time holder that was of my present. It hovered on top of the table. It had many areas where it could join securely to my past as if my past was reaching up to my present, making it able to adhere. It had not become like concrete. My present is still forming so it had not hardened yet.

Next from a section atop of the time cylinder came a disk made of a stunning white light with lightning moving inside of it. I knew this was my future. This disk had very few places to adhere to my present. It was amazing, shocking, breathtaking, embarrassing, and surreal to see my life with my accomplishments, failures, and secrets all exposed. The Lord and everyone in this war room were looking at my life. My future was being considered and mapped out because of a big trouble that was coming.

I understood that the table was a war table. Jesus was using it while carefully looking over my life to help me succeed. Knowing that He was helping me "win" made me so happy! I went running up to Him, and I hugged Him from His back. I was so happy to see Him and to touch Him! The angel who had been steadying me was very upset. I could understand the angel's thoughts were, *"What are you doing to Him?"*

My answer seemed to fill the whole room as it was truth.

"I need Him!"

There is a love language called touch. I don't have much of that love language necessarily on the earth. My husband wishes that I had that love language a little more. In Heaven, we all have it. I held to Jesus, and I was not in a hurry to let go.

He turned around, and I could see He was very serious. He was not upset that I had hugged Him, but I had not been brought to the war room for a hug. He welcomed me to stand right beside Himself and began showing me my life.

He said, *"Life!"*

I could suddenly see a light that was mine. In the past it was a darker color, but it kept becoming lighter as my timeline continued. Beside Him I was in perfect balance. I could see the time when I accepted Jesus as my Savior, causing my path's light to join His. He was personally showing me my life. I could see my past and all the yucky, bumpy things in it. He was not really interested in that time as it was in concrete. Anybody got a yucky past? It doesn't matter! That was yesterday. That's done. You can't change it. Learn from it.

Then I had my present. I could see the bright light of the Lord mapped out. From what I knew (which was nothing really) I thought I was doing pretty well in my present. At least it was lit with a white light. My present was close to the Lord's light. But then I realized that if I was with the Lord perfectly, I wouldn't be able to see my light at all.

The scripture that comes to mind is, *"He must increase and I must decrease."*[5] All of a sudden, I was not really impressed with my present, which made me want to really help the Lord with my future. He knew my thoughts, and He liked that I was teachable.

The Lord was trying to land my future onto the other two times. As He removed a section and was adding a slice, I could tell that He was going to re-route me.

Suddenly I could see why my light was so bright. It was because His light was right beside my light. I could also see that He was getting ready to separate our paths. My light was going very dim. That was bad! My present was brighter than my future.

I could see that the Lord's path was going to go the hard way. My path originally was going to go the hard way with the Lord too. Hard doesn't mean bad; it only means hard. But He was going to change my path, and He was instructing the angels how to change it to make it go down and around by the waters. It was the easy way with no problems.

I saw what He was doing, and I started arguing.

"No! That's not what I want, Lord! I need to go the way that You are going!"

I could hear the thoughts of the angels. They were wanting me to be sent away. I began shouting at the angels. (I think as I write this, *not wise!*) I felt they didn't understand and weren't on my side!

I grabbed Jesus' arm and asked Him, *"Why are You letting them do that? What have I done wrong? I don't want to go that way! Lord, I need You!"*

I was a hysterical mess! The angel who had brought me into the room tried to get me to let go of the Lord while I continued to beg Jesus, *"Please Lord, with all that I am, do not cast me from You!"*

Suddenly, everything was silent and still. The angel stepped back. The Lord was looking deeply at me as tears streamed down my face, and I shook my head no at Him.

The angels were highly upset. *Nobody* argues with the Creator—His strategies are perfect! But my heart would not be settled. I knew they could all hear my heart, and I let it speak. *"You made me to be with You!"*

I looked at the table, *"Remember, I almost didn't find You! Lord, don't send me in a way without You. What if I get lost and can never find You again?"*[6]

The Lord was going to change my path. Whatever direction I was going, for reasons I didn't understand, He was getting ready to change my path. I wasn't going to go the way of the Lord, which was a hard way. He was changing my path to go an easy way.

My heart continued, *"Please, Savior, don't change my path! I need to go the way that You go. I'm Your favorite one. I always want to be on Your team. I want to be where You are!"*

He looked at me and He said, *"If you go this hard way, I could lose you."*

I felt it, His great concern for me. Something was just up ahead that was going to cause me to be surrounded by the enemy. The darkness was going to be so great that my prophetic giftings would be silenced. A hardness that would cause me to doubt everything and bring unthinkable fear was waiting to hijack me. Jesus was waging war against the enemy and would not allow my life to be endangered. Changing my path was for my good.

I began to understand the battle. Jesus was fighting for me.

I said to Him, *"You'll never lose me! Nothing can ever make me forget You. I know I am Your favorite one. You're never going to lose me! Never!"*

He studied my face. As I looked into His great eyes, I saw the amazing gift that He had given me at the beginning of my times. I could choose. The gift of choice is an amazing gift that God never removes. He is not a manipulator. Rather, He is an equipper.

As He began to speak, I knew this was the most important thing that He had ever told me. He said again, *"I could lose you."*

I understood why I was in the room. I understood that I am so important to Him. I nodded to Him and knew that ultimately the choice was mine.[7] The room was silent. The angels were no help in my choosing. I looked at the table as my path was being grooved to go the easy way. I made up my mind. Suddenly the new pathway stopped. I chose to go the hard way. Jesus would be there on my hard path even if I couldn't see, hear, or feel Him. I understood that a real war was coming.

He nodded. He let me choose, and the table quickly readjusted. The angel was immediately by my side. I could sense that the angels were no longer agitated but now were pleased.

My path lit back up to go the hard way. I knew that I needed to be right in step with Jesus for my light to remain a light. My past, present, and future all melted into the war table. All three parts came together. My times rose up off the table and returned to the shape of the pizza disk and then reentered the cylinder.

I looked at Jesus. I was smart enough to ask for something before I left. *"Have mercy on me, Lord!"*

I watched His eyes of fire and knew that He delighted to grant me great mercy. The angel's wings opened, and suddenly I was back driving on the freeway at 55 miles per hour. Oh my gosh!

I was shocked! I slammed on the brakes and pulled over to the side of the road as fast as I could. I had no idea where I was, but I instantly started yelling: *"No! No, no! I'll take the easy way! Lord, I'll take the easy way!"*

Suddenly I was in a compete panic! I chose wrong! I'd rather have the easy way. I saw that hard way. I don't want to go that way. The easy path was great—no attack, no enemy, no worries. Just live and die in my sleep.

I told Him, *"You were right; You are always right!"*

My mind was whirling. If the Lord said He thought He could lose me, then, *hello,* I could be lost! I was physically shaking. As the cars whizzed by, I began pounding on the steering wheel. Fear was gripping my heart. It was just a matter of time, and then I would be lost.

Suddenly I felt the calming of the Holy Spirit. He whispered to my heart, *"The hard time is not here yet. You will be ready, and you will be granted mercy. Pick up your cross and follow Jesus!"*[8]

Somehow, I made it home and waited excitedly to tell Mike. The choice had been made, and I was going to go the hard way. Mike was very supportive. He assured me that many great people have taken very hard paths and are with Jesus today. In my prayer time, I felt like the ones who will live in Jesus' house are the ones who took the hard way. This brought me a measure of comfort and resolve.

If you've got a hard thing happening in your life, remember Jesus took the hard way. If you want to take the way that your light and His are on the same path, then you are going to have to take the hard way. If the hard way produces something that I can turn around and give to my children or grandchildren, isn't it better that I take the hard way and be able to help them through it? How many things in my life have been so bad?

And I can also go and minister to someone who is struggling in that hard thing because the Lord took me through it. He can use me to help somebody else because of a hard thing. My past really was just a foundation to bring in my present and to help form my future.

I've set my heart to not be a complainer.[9] I asked the Lord for the hard way because that's the way He was going. My spirit was in control, and it knew exactly how to choose. I can trust that so much more than I can trust my mind, will, or emotions.

Now, I have a rule in my life. If I can stop the first complaint, I have killed them all.[10] The next one isn't going to happen if I don't let the first one have its way. So instead of complaining, I try extra hard to be thankful. Off the top of my head can I quickly think of twenty things to be thankful for? Once I think of twenty, it's easy to find one hundred. It's that first twenty that are the hardest. Once I begin thanking Him, the complaining can't succeed at shutting me down.

In Heaven we're going to look back on the times when God taught us about being thankful and not complaining, cherishing the hard way. We will know He took us on that path intentionally, for His glory. I'm very glad that God is in the hard places because we don't realize our need for God when everything is easy. It's when things are difficult that I say, *"Take both my hands and help me walk through this, because I can't see, I can't hear, and I can't feel anything."* And He is there in that hard place.[11]

Now, to answer the question that everyone asks. Did I go through the hard way yet? I will answer yes and no. Many people think the hard way was when I went to hell (see the book, *The Hell Conspiracy*). At first, I thought that maybe that was it. It was not. Seeing hell and burning did not turn me away from God. I knew that only His way saves.

There was a time that was very dangerous. I almost chose to leave the light and make my own way. That vision is in the chapter titled "Go." However, I won't know for sure until I am with Jesus again. Therefore, I live like I am at war and remember that the enemy has a plan to steal me away from Jesus.[12]

Maybe living this way is the safest way to live. I know the hard way is a path to eternal life that will bring great results![13]

NOTES

1. John 17:24
2. John 14:2
3. 2 Timothy 4:5
4. Acts 1:7
5. John 3:30
6. Matthew 7:14
7. Psalm 23:4
8. Matthew 16:24-26
9. Philippians 2:14
10. John 6:43, James 5:9
11. Deuteronomy 31:8
12. Ephesians 6:11
13. Matthew 7:14

CHAPTER 11

GO

"He answered, 'Yes, sir, I will go and work.' But he did not go."

—MATTHEW 21:30 ERV

One of the most important lessons the Lord taught me was during a trip abroad. The Lord invited me to go to India and hug the lepers for Him. It all sounded so wonderful on this side of the ocean. I was being chosen to do something extraordinary and that feels good in the flesh. When Mike and I were invited by an Indian pastor to preach and share about Heaven and hell, I was so excited as I felt that I was living a "suddenly moment." I raised money for the trip and gave my itinerary to everyone who donated. I wanted prayer from them, particularly on Monday, when I would be at the leper colony.

India is an amazing country with multitudes of beautiful people who need to know Jesus. I was invited to share my testimony at many venues. We saw numerous people choose Jesus and repent of following false gods. The culture differences between India and America were vast, but the gospel of Jesus Christ and His salvation is universal. I was not intimidated by anything until Sunday.

On Sunday I preached in three small villages. The last village was an extremely poor one in which I shared about eternity. The pastor in charge of the region had appointed evangelists over these villages that were in need of the gospel. The majority of those who came to listen were not saved.

I was dressed in Indian attire. Most of the women's clothes are very stunning with brilliant colors. My first full day in India was spent shopping for the correct clothing. The pastor had told me ahead of time that western wear would not be suitable to preach the gospel because many consider it immodest. My task of finding clothing was hard due to my color restrictions. I only wear black and white, something I began in 2013 when the Lord spoke to me. He said, *"If you live a black and white life, I will anoint you when you speak."* Some have argued that He only meant it figuratively, but I disagree. I could only find a few things in these colors, as red and vibrant pinks are the national favorite.

The outfit I wore was black with a small amount of white and made of a unique material. It was pretty, but uncomfortable like wearing plastic. It would not breathe like the cotton attire I had worn on other days. It had long sleeves and a high neck. The dress part came down close to my knees and had two slits on either side up to my thigh. There were also loose fitting, one size fits all pantaloons that tied at my ankles and waist. It also came with a long scarf that draped from one side of me to the other, almost touching the ground. India was sweltering, and the attire made me miserably hot. I have always struggled in the heat so I was excited when I finally finished and could get into the air-conditioned car. According to the schedule, we were done for the day.

I was looking forward to a cold shower and a chance to put my foot up. Unfortunately, I had injured my foot right before leaving for India. I had a four-inch cut on the side of it so I was babying it, and I wore sandals to allow it to breathe.

Suddenly, the pastor had the driver turn around. I asked where we were going, and he explained that the leper colony was just a short distance away so we would stop there before returning home. The car was not available tomorrow, so instead we would go there that night.

I was instantly filled with panic. I did not want to go to the leper colony. I had a plan, and it was for tomorrow. I wondered, should I tell him why I didn't want to go tonight?

1. The intercessors would be praying back home tomorrow.
2. I had planned on wearing a bandage on my hurt foot along with socks and tennis shoes.
3. I had planned on wearing much simpler attire as the lepers mostly have only the clothes on their backs.

4. I had planned on having already eaten. I was very hungry.

5. I had planned on bringing gifts for them.

6. I planned on being *ready!*

Even as I considered my reasons, I heard Mike tell the pastor that this would be perfect. I was in a state of inner turmoil.

When we arrived, I was shocked. The leper colony was surrounded on three sides by a dump. There were fires burning inside of the dump, so it smelled absolutely terrible, and it was filthy everywhere. The compound was surrounded by a tall rock wall with a small gate for entrance. We could go in, but if the lepers were to venture outside of the wall, the townspeople would kill them. Getting visitors in this place was a *big deal.*

The pastor explained that when the government originally set up the colony, the area was rural, but as the towns grew, room for a city dump was a necessity. A decision was made to put it around the compound. The people across the street were some of the poorest in the area, but they were terrified of the lepers and did not want to catch the disease that would place them inside the compound. These outside people would kill the lepers out of fear for themselves and their families. He shared that the Church pays for the lepers to get the needed medical treatment, because the government will not.

The lepers in the colony were confined to the compound along with their entire family. Their pastor, an evangelist, willingly entered with his family to help the colony meet Jesus. He went in disease-free, but he, too, can never leave because the townspeople fear that he also has leprosy.

Although this was utterly tragic, at the moment I didn't care. I didn't want to be there. What about my foot? What about the original plan?

When we walked inside, I was very surprised. It was clean and tidy. The tall walls actually kept out much of the smell of the burning dump. The pastor of the compound met us and welcomed us. The first little hut was the church, and he explained that everyone would be coming soon. He was so thankful that we had changed our schedule to include them. He explained that many will not come to the leper colony. I wanted to yell and tell them that the deal was off.

As I looked down the pathway, I saw a woman dragging her body on the dirt. She was yelling/moaning to get my attention. Her hair was standing on end, and she was trying to point her hand, missing four fingers, at me. I panicked. Others were trying to walk with a stick, children came running, and the woman with the crazy hair kept yelling.

I looked at the pastor and explained that I needed to use the restroom. I thought that would get me out of the gate that I had entered. Instead he spoke to a teenage girl who looked like she did not have leprosy. She led me around the back of the church to another pathway through a small gate into the community potty. I did not know if this was the women's or if it served everyone. The "toilet" consisted of a hole in the ground, and the area around it was wet but clean.

I was trying to think fast, but nothing was coming to mind. I was scared, tired, hot, beyond stressed, and now I really did have to go.

I tried to hike up the dress while dropping the pantaloons and balancing the scarf. The scarf dipped into what I will call the leprosy liquid first, and then my dress somehow also dipped its hem into the liquid. Then I lost my balance, and the pantaloons got wet while I tried to catch myself. Finally, the leprosy liquid splashed onto my cut foot.

Now there you have it. I yelled out something like, *"You have got to be kidding me!"* The girl began answering me in her language. I quickly composed myself and opened the door. She reached in and took a ladle of water from a nearby bucket to rinse the area for me.

I faked a smile and motioned for her to run along, which she did. I watched her go back up the pathway toward the little church. My mind was whirling. There was no running water that I could see. There was no soap to wash my hands and, more importantly, my foot. I was positive that I had contracted leprosy!

I realize this all sounds funny, but trust me, I have never laughed about it.

In my desperate confusion, I made a quick decision: I was going home. I was leaving India that day. I could land in the USA in 13-plus hours and get myself to the closest hospital to get a shot. I would tell Mike that we needed to leave immediately, get into the car, and wait until the others joined me.

As I was walking back toward the church hut, Jesus encountered me.[1] The only way to explain it is that an office dropped out of Heaven with Him in it. It dropped on top of me so that I was surrounded by this heavenly office. The room was perfectly square shaped and made of a type of white fog. I could see through the fog in the same way that if you try hard you can see through white sheer curtains. It was difficult to see the path that I had walked, but it was not impossible.

I was so excited to see Jesus, and I was sure that He would help me get back home. Suddenly, His thoughts were very loud inside of the heavenly office. He wasn't there to get me home. He was there to encourage me, to infuse His strength in me, and to give me a pep talk like a coach gives to an athlete. He was looking forward to me hugging the lepers.

This was not at all what I wanted!

I felt like He was giving me something that would let them feel His love through my arms. At that moment, I was not willing to accept it. This surprised Him. He looked at me, and I knew He could see all of my fear. I thought He would give me a pass because this task seemed insurmountable. But that was not going to happen.

He said, *"I sent you here for this."*

I responded, *"No!"* I shook my head and kept repeating the same word over and over.

Jesus looked very serious and was trying to calm me with His explanations. He began: *"India has many false gods and needs the truth. I desire to make India a sign and a wonder and for there to be more children of the Kingdom now."*

I understood that He desired to make India a Christian nation because otherwise many, too many, precious people would perish.

I said, *"No!"* again and again. I did not care about the individual, let alone the nation. I felt that I was at risk. I could not see my own pride.

He said, *"The lepers are the absolute least in position, and My eyes and ears are always attentive to them."*

In my great pride, I just kept telling Him no.

He stopped and looked directly at me. It was not a calming look. I knew that He is not accustomed to His servants, ones who have had such privilege as myself, to address Him with such blatant disregard. He began shaking His head like He was thinking the word "no." As I waited, my own thoughts became crystal clear.

I said to Jesus, *"Those people have leprosy, and they are going to make me sick. Don't you care that they will make me sick?"*

Jesus replied so loudly, and yet it was a mere whisper, *"You think that I don't care about them! You think that they have leprosy because of Me?"*[2]

There was an uneasy silence as I came to grips with my own thoughts. I believed that they had this because Jesus wanted them to have it. Otherwise, wouldn't He have already healed them?

He looked out past the fog and said the scariest thing. He said, *"I sent you here for this. I sent you here for them."*[3]

There was another lengthy silence. I was so uncomfortable. I felt totally alive, and I shook with the nearness of Jesus. Everything He spoke was complete *truth*. And I knew it.

His eyes looked at me with a mixture of grief and disbelief. He said, *"If you will not do this, you will not hear 'well done, good and faithful servant.'"*[4]

Suddenly, instead of saying "no" in disobedience, I was saying "no" about the idea of not hearing "well done." How could this be? I am a favored child of God. He has taken me to Heaven many times and shown me remarkable things. He has used me more times than I can count to share His truths of my experience in hell. How could it be that in this one act of disobedience, I could lose it all?

I began to run toward Him in hopes of grabbing on to His mercy. As I got closer to Him, the office disappeared, and I was running on the pathway. I ran with a decision I needed to make. Either I would tell Mike to get me back to the USA, or I would hug the lepers.

As I turned the corner, I saw that the people were gathered outside the church and sitting on the dirt. The men sat on one side and the women on the other. There was a baby just learning to walk who was moving from left to right visiting both men and women. This child did not see leprosy but was surrounded in a community where he felt safe and loved. Everyone loved the child deeply.

I saw Mike out of the corner of my eye, but I looked for the woman with the crazy hair. Her body was deformed from the leprosy. It had eaten away at her joints and deformed her limbs, making it impossible for her to walk. She also had a sunken face on her right side, another terrible outcome of the disease. I ran directly to her and knelt down. The right side of my face was touching the right side of hers. She was taken aback. She tried to tell me no. I held on to her so tightly and cried. I held on as if my life depended on it, because it did. I first felt the pain from the intense fear leave me with each sob that shook my body.

As I held her, my fear turned into great shame that I had not considered her life worth bringing the gift that Jesus wanted her to have. As I held her, I kept asking her to forgive me, but she couldn't understand a word. She relaxed as I was physically stronger than her, but it was as if she was receiving something. I prayed it was *nothing* from me but what Jesus had deposited into me, what He wanted to flow into her as I held her in my arms.[5]

I took off the bangle bracelets I was wearing (my wrists are much larger than the typical Indian woman) and slid them onto her deformed hands. Giving jewelry is a sign that you believe this person to be of great value. Now the tears flowed freely from us both.

I stood up and moved to the next woman and I held her while we cried. She too tried to tell me not to hug her, but I did it anyway. I do not know why she cried, but I wept from the exhaustion that my body felt as it moved from disobedience into obedience.[6] Did you know that disobedience is extremely tiring while obedience brings life? She too finally relaxed, and soon it was as if I was hugging a dear friend.

By now, Mike was hugging the men, and the church was all about hugging. I hugged each leper. The mother of the toddler held on to the child as he was the only one who would not let me come so close. I understood as I also had a grandbaby about that same age.

I was humbled as we began. These people had brought out the few chairs inside the community for us to sit on while they sat in the dirt. They waited for us to teach them from the word of God. I spoke on the scripture about loving one another the way that Jesus does.[7] I commended them for doing just that!

Before we knew it, the pastor said we had to leave. Mike and I persuaded him to let us stay longer, and we visited each little hut. The community held a little over 40 people, including one woman due to deliver a baby soon. The pastor explained how they have a few blended families because when a dad from one family dies and a mom from a different family dies, the remaining couple would marry each other and the new family would be whole again. That explained the large gap in the ages of the husbands and wives.

These precious people had nothing and yet were willing to share everything. We sat on the floor with them and listened to their needs. And these were truly needs. They asked for blankets as they only had a few in the compound. They asked for a large cooking pot because they cook and eat as a community. They asked for rice and spices. They needed new roofs on their huts because their space was unlivable during the rainy season. One teenage girl asked for a brush to care for the women's hair. The only brush they had was a small broken piece, which she showed me for proof of her request.

I wrote each request down and assured them that I could get the majority of the items, but I would need help to figure out the roof problems.

As we talked, in no time at all I could no longer see the leprosy. Instead I saw the beautiful smiles they shared. I gave away much jewelry. With each piece given, they all celebrated the person receiving the gift.

Sadly, I ran out of jewelry too soon. The first lady to whom I had given the bangles got my attention and motioned for me to take the bracelets and give them to the other women. My heart was filled with such love and admiration toward her. She knew the custom and wanted her "children" to feel valuable. She was the oldest person in the compound and had been born in it. She was a mighty Christian woman who took her role very seriously. When many may have been bitter toward God, she was far from it. I have never met a more selfless woman, and I will never forget her.

We left and talked all the way to our hotel about how precious all the people were. We also made arrangements for the pastor to bring everything they had requested back to them. Everything except for the roofing. This need was more than just paying for a new roof. We had to find people willing to enter the compound and do the work, and many of the structures themselves were in need of extensive repairs.

We left full. We were full of the love of God. These people had given us so much more than we could have ever given them.[8] Mike told us that he felt as if the Lord had let us spend time with "The Royalty of the Earth." I had to agree.

When we returned home from India, I went on a fast. My goal was to find out what had gone wrong. I *never* wanted my God to have to challenge me with my eternal safety again. I began my fast right away to rid myself of distractions so that I could hear Him clearly whenever He might choose to speak.

Very soon, He put the following impressions into my heart, which will take many words to try and explain.

One issue was that I was not in control. I did not like the schedule changing, and although it was upsetting for me it was necessary for the timetable of the Lord.

I had a wound on my foot that really worried me, but it was a necessary tool needed for the heavenly test.[9]

I was wearing clothes that made me very uncomfortable but were needed to help me achieve the end result. As Mike had seen, we were with people most precious to Jesus and dressing up to meet them was totally acceptable.

I had figured these out on my own, but I needed the Lord's help to know exactly what had caused me to walk in blatant disobedience to Him.

I was shocked by His answer!

He said, *"You were filled with fear, but in the past I have used you in spite of your fear. You were filled with pride, but in the past I have used you in spite of your pride. In India, you were also filled with your opinions."*

There was silence as I processed these truths.

His understandings came again: *"These three together will take you away from Me and My plans. Beware of your opinions!"*

As I write this, I still feel the shock.[10] A dangerous combination—fear, pride, and opinion. In India, I had the opinion that I must have contracted leprosy. This led me to a series of solutions, all of which were outside of my God-given task. All I could think about in my panic was that I had to leave immediately. My weak little opinion was going to destroy everything the Lord had planned.[11]

Suddenly, I understood the vision from years before where the Lord had tried to change my path to the easy one. He knew my fear and pride and the deadly combination of adding my opinion to the mix could cause me to fall away. I never want to come so close to being lost ever again!

I am often reminded of how Jesus said, "Nevertheless not My will, but Yours, be done," as He waited in the garden.[12] I can, even now, hear the Holy Spirit encourage me, "Deny yourself, pick up your cross and follow God."[13]

NOTES

1. Luke 24:35

2. Psalm 135:6

3. Matthew 25:40

4. Matthew 25:23

5. 2 Thessalonians 1:7

6. Isaiah 40:29

7. John 13:34

8. Acts 20:35

9. James 1:2-3

10. Proverbs 3:5-7

11. 1 John 2:17

12 Luke 22:42

13. Matthew 16:24-26

CHAPTER 12

---◆◆---

HEAVEN'S STABLES

"Being confident of this very thing, that
He who has begun a good work in you will
complete it until the day of Jesus Christ."

—PHILIPPIANS 1:6

Heaven has many animals and quite the selection of amazing creatures that are not on the earth.[1] In Heaven, I like to watch the sky as there are many more winged creatures. They are all simply amazing! We can communicate with the creatures in Heaven, so there is such a mutual appreciation for the uniqueness in all of us.

I have visited Heaven's stables twice. On my first visit, I was walking with Jesus, and He pointed to dogs running toward a magnificent, massive, round building. They were running ahead of the

Lord in excitement of the day and what was happening there. The young puppies did not follow the older dogs but instead came right to the Lord. They jumped and twirled as a show of their genuine affection. I understood them because of their actions, but in Heaven I also understood their hearts. They wanted to play with Jesus and use themselves to bring Him happiness.

He reached down and all of the puppies tried to jump into His arms. A small brown and tan one jumped up the fastest and caused the Lord to laugh. The others all sat down. Not at all what I was expecting. They just waited because they knew that their turn would come at just the right time. I was amazed that the puppies were so mature. I bent down and picked up a little white and tan dog. Tears began to form in my eyes. Immediately memories flooded my mind. As a child, I had a little dog similar to the one I was holding. I loved the puppy deeply. Its name was Snowball. My brother became very sick as soon as Snowball came to live with us. It didn't take long to realize that he was allergic to the puppy, so Snowball was sent to my aunt's farm about an hour from our house. Unfortunately, Snowball was not used to free ranging and was hit by a car and killed. I cried countless tears at the news.

Before the water gathered in my eyes remembering Snowball, this puppy communicated how much it loved *me*. I asked through heart communication how it could love me so much. The puppy said that she loved me because I first loved her. I asked her name, and she was very proud to tell me that her name was Snowball. Then she licked my hand and jumped out of my arms to run down the stone path toward the stable. Jesus kissed the one that He was holding, and it too ran after Snowball. It was all so exciting. I had many questions about Snowball, but I did not ask the Lord if that was my dog. I just knew she was! And as I watched the puppies run toward the building, my excitement grew, wondering where we all were going and why.

The pathway to the stables was wonderful. It was a cobblestone walkway made of living stones much like those on the stairwell in the "Summoned Celebration" chapter. The walkway itself was so happy that the Lord was traveling along it. And the fields alongside were stunning with yellow and white flowers that all waved as if a mighty wind was blowing. They, like the puppies, were using themselves to bring happiness to Jesus. As we got closer, I heard and felt a strong vibration on the ground, much like a drum beat.

In the stable, the horses were all stamping their hooves and making a gleeful horse noise. I had never seen such beautiful, big horses. They were using their strength to beat out a welcome for the King! It was such a happy occasion. The stable had a vented and round top, but the structure was held in place by three pillars of light at the center. Structurally this was not possible, but in Heaven all things are possible. Coming out of the light was crystal clear water, which the horses could walk up to and get a drink without bending down.

The horses walked past the Lord and bent their necks down low while Jesus clapped with joy for their quickly orchestrated parade. As I watched, there were many other animals that had come to the stable to see what the Lord was highlighting. There were also many angels there. The angels were laughing with the horses, combing their manes, braiding their tails, and letting the horses choose jewelry. Seeing the angels place jewels on the horses much like we wear bracelets and necklaces, I became happier too. Of course, the Lord has more than enough treasures for everyone and everything to be beautified in splendor.

I was instantly drawn to look up, and there she stood—my horse. The Lord introduced us. Her name is Freedom.

Let me back up a bit. When I was pregnant with our first daughter, my parents, my husband, Mike, and I were in an old five and dime store. I looked up and hanging high was a picture of a great white horse. It was a painting on black velvet. It was not a popular type of picture as the era of black velvet paintings was long past. Still I became so excited about the picture because I knew that this horse was mine. Now mind you, I am not a horse rider or owner. I had been placed on ponies as a child for photo ops, but until that moment I never cared about horses.

I said, *"I need that picture!"*

My husband was shocked, as I had never shown any interest in horses. He asked me where would I hang such a picture, and I told him it would go perfectly in our bedroom. Mike shared how he didn't think this overpowering picture was a fit for our small place.

I surprised myself at my insistence that I *needed* that picture. I had no money, so I asked my dad for it, and he quickly had the shopkeeper bring it down. Several employees came to help with the ladder. It had a lot of dust on it. They wanted to know who was buying the old painting that had hung there for ages and were somewhat surprised to see me, someone who knows nothing at all about horses.

That was 35 years ago, and the painting has always had a place of honor in my home. I spent many early morning hours staring at the horse and always being excited that someday I would ride such a magnificent animal. As Freedom came close, I realized that she was the horse of the picture. I had known, long before I was saved, that I had a magnificent horse and we would ride together in Heaven.

Instead of being afraid of the massive animal, I reached up and could not touch the top of her back. She bent down and let me hug her neck. I could not stop the tears of joy. I had so many questions! Snowball was there jumping around my feet and barking as if she was singing a song. Freedom joined in and then I began singing with the two of them.

My "sound" came out of me. It was not words, but the sound that distinguishes me from everyone else. Each of our sounds is as unique as our fingerprints. I am not positive, but I think the lyrics we were singing were:

"I love You, Lord, and I lift my voice to worship You. Oh my soul, rejoice! Take joy my King in what You hear. May it be a sweet, sweet sound in Your ear."

Next thing I knew, everything was singing as the massive horses stamped out this song. I was so overjoyed!

The Lord asked me if I was ready to ride with Freedom. I couldn't wait! I stepped back and looked at her. She was so beautiful and white, like a very light blonde color. She had blue eyes like me, and her favorite color was also blue. She had sparkling gems tied into her mane with matching ones braided into her tail. I looked around for how I should get on her, but instantly the Lord put me on her with just His thoughts. None of the horses had saddles, bits, or stirrups. These items are not needed to ride in Heaven as somehow horses become one with their riders.

Freedom took me over to where the angels were hoisting banners on long poles. They looked very official. We were to choose a banner that best fit us. Freedom had already studied the banners and requested that we look at her three favorites. I was amazed at how similar our preferences were. The banners were made of amazing heavenly material that was alive, and as we looked, each banner straightened itself out so that I could see it. These were warrior banners. Each one had an attribute of God expressed in it to declare a truth of God in the midst of war.

I told Freedom I was proud of her and asked if she had a favorite one of the three—Patience, Kindness, and Goodness. As we looked to Jesus for His help, we instantly both knew that we would ride for Jesus because of His great patience. With that knowledge, the Lord agreed and the banner of Patience was fitted to us.

Throughout all my supernatural visits, I have always identified with the Lord through His patience.[2] Today as I recall these visions and daily life experiences, I am reminded again and again of this truth throughout my life.

Freedom walked me over to where the angels were going to dress her in armor. The Lord asked if I would like to ride with her to experience the difference of before and after the armor was fitted. I was again very excited.

Freedom began running out of the stables. She ran very fast and kept accelerating. In an instant we were at a cliff. I grabbed hold of her mane at first, thinking that I had to be sure I didn't fall off, but I was wrong. Somehow because of the will of Jesus for us to be a team, I would not fall off of Freedom. I was filled with awe at her great strength and agility. Before I understood, she jumped off the cliff, and we were flying. She is one of the winged creatures in Heaven. I was so excited that I could not stop laughing! She took me higher and I was filled with so much gratitude that the Lord had tied me to such a wonderful gift!

Finally, when we landed the Lord was sitting with the smaller animals telling them stories of the horses. He was smiling at us and nodded for us to be fitted with armor. I was instantly beside Freedom and in front of me were many pieces of armor for my horse. The angels helped me dress her.

This day was very special for Freedom. Today she was becoming a warhorse for the Lord of Hosts.[3] She had many pieces of the heavenly material attached to her. The material was not only beautiful but impenetrable. The material could change color and could even camouflage when needed. Once she was dressed, Freedom appeared even larger and stronger. I was so glad to have been there to watch the transformation.

The angels then handed me my articles to put on as well. On previous occasions when I visited Heaven, I had been given specific pieces of armor. It wasn't until that moment in the stable that

I realized that these gifts were my armor. Over the course of different visits, I had become equipped. Now all those pieces were being fit together to prepare me for the coming battle.

First, an amazing, stunning dress allowed me to dance with the Lord so I would know how He moves. Then a tiara identified me as a child of the King and gave me wisdom. A ring on my right pointer finger gave me authority to mark His words. My feet were given a pair of wonderful sandals that lit when I walked the correct path but turned dark when I went the wrong way. Around my shoulders draped a cloak of the same camouflage material as Freedom's armor. As long as I remained humble, the material would keep me hidden from evil eyes.[4]

Attached to my clothing was an Arabian-shaped sword with a hilt carrying a red, blue, and green stone. The blue stone represented the glory of the Lamb and 144,000.[5] The green stone was given for acceptance of godly finances because I chose not to serve both God and money.[6] I agreed that the Lord owns all the silver and gold and all I have is His. The red was earned from knowledge that the blood of Christ has washed away not only my sins, but also the sins of the lost if they will allow it because Jesus desires that many be with Him.[7] I carry a wound from the sword of the Lord; I hurt that people do not know Him and His truth. I have a continually increasing, burning passion for more truth and holiness.

I was given a shield of faith, which came by the knowledge of the Cross. Around my neck was placed a necklace that identified my callings in the Lord. I was fitted with many purses, which are the ministries entrusted to me by the Lord. Perfume was applied to strengthen my prayer life. Little flowers were placed in my hair representing the fruit of the Spirit.[8] I was given a mirror to look into my own eyes and to allow God to speak to me. I was also given mini candies representing the gifts of the Spirit. Into my hands were placed a checkbook with the authority to write checks for the purpose of letting others encounter Jesus and a pen to write down what I saw.

Although I had received these pieces of armor in many different visions, they came together as the angels dressed Freedom and me. We all have heavenly armor the Lord desires to give us. Our armor in the Lord may be different, but we are each equipped perfectly for the Lord's calling.

When I was finally completely dressed in my armor, I was placed once again on Freedom by our mutual understanding and acceptance of each other. I was handed the banner of Patience that now felt very lightweight. I could carry it or place it in a special holder on my right side. All the horses arranged themselves on both sides of the walkway. When the Lord of Hosts made a large noise like that of a trumpet blast, Freedom began marching, and the other horses began stomping out their acceptance of her and ultimately me. I was in such awe of understanding that not only was Freedom a part of the army of the Lord of Hosts, but so was I.[9]

Before this vision, I didn't know that I was part of God's army even though my spirit knew it from the time I saw the picture of the horse. God was always at work bringing me all the pieces of armor I would need. I wouldn't have been complete as a warrior without Freedom. We can trust that God is equipping us for whatever wonderful adventure He is going to ask us to do. That equipping can begin even before we know Jesus as our Savior. As He promised, He will complete the good work He began in us![10]

My second visit to the stable could not have been more different. When I arrived, the stable was completely full of horses already in large groups. More horses were flying in from everywhere and landing in the fields. They were grouped in specific categories according to the banner under which they rode. There were miles and miles of horses. They went for as far as my eyes could see.

The atmosphere was tense. There was a great seriousness surrounding the upcoming ride. No horse talked to another. The angels were quickly checking the heavenly materials on both the horses and the riders. As the last groups of horses arrived into the ranks, the only sound I could hear was of my own breathing. Everyone was intently listening.

Suddenly, the Lord flew into the area on His massive horse.[11] He lit up the whole sky. Everyone saw Him at the same time like a great flash of lightning. There came a cheer so loud that it shook everything. Then a wind like I have never known lifted all the horses at the same time into the sky with the Lord. I knew the wind was the Holy Spirit. He had not come like a gentleman but rather like the unstoppable force that He is. It was apparent that Holy Spirit was *extremely* strong!

Again, there was a great silence, and then the Father spoke. We could hear Him from His throne. The words that He spoke were not English, but their meaning was crystal clear. He blessed His Son and told Him to go get His bride.[12]

Again, there was a silence as everyone waited for Jesus to speak.

From His mouth came a sound. It is hard to explain it, but it was as if it was a trumpet, an alarm, a groan, a shot, and a roar. It was together, but separate enough to know that I had never heard anything like it. In an instant, everything changed. We were thrust out of Heaven with a force like no other. I was not prepared for the jolt. This ride was not at all like my first ride.

Once we left Heaven, every evil force came against us to break us apart. We had to work at staying together. We were a complete unit together, so to take one of us out would have taken us both out. My mind was whirling. I was a part of the army of the Lord, and I did not want to let Him down. As we raced, I wrapped my hands several times in Freedom's mane, praying that I would stay atop her.

When the dim light of earth was hazy in the distance, I looked down at Freedom and saw that the heavenly material had hidden her. She was now black; it was not the color black but darkness. The material had camouflaged her. She was prepared to go into the greatest darkness. As I looked around, I could no longer see the other horses or their riders because of their camouflage.

Freedom was not afraid, or at least she did not act that way. As we plunged into the darkness, my thoughts were attacked.[13] I could hear the enemy telling me that I should not be here, that I was a sinner, and that I would deny the Lord my God. I remembered the pieces of my armor and began using each piece, beginning with my tiara. I also began praying in tongues for Freedom.[14] If I was being attacked, then so was she. I then prayed for all the teams.[15]

The battle grew more intense the deeper we dove into the darkness. My legs throbbed from the pressure of pushing myself into Freedom's body. She was so strong that I knew she would crush whatever met. If I had not known her before, I would have been extremely intimated by her. I kept repeating the same phrase over and over: *"Don't fall!"*

All of a sudden, I was back in my kitchen having prayer time. I was shaken, to say the least. I understood that Jesus has been preparing me for years to be in His army. I was in a place of honor riding with the Lord, and He trusted me to be in His army. Because He made me to be a new creation in Christ, I would not betray Him. Because I was already equipped with my heavenly armor, I knew that if I had not done everything to stay on Freedom, I would have betrayed the Lord and become like satan who was, at one time, a trusted leader in the Lord's army. I knew that if I fell off, I was against God and for satan. While in the battle, I had to keep control of my mind, will, and emotions. I had to trust God. I had to believe. Once we are maturely equipped, we have to do everything He tells us to do or we will fall away.[16]

As unsettling as this is, it is the danger we all face—my choices today could cause me to fall on that day. Therefore, I pay attention to each day and what I need to do in it. I do today what the Lord has asked of me. This is what we are all called to as His children.

NOTES

1. Isaiah 66:2
2. 2 Peter 3:9
3. Proverbs 21:31
4. 1 Peter 5:6-7
5. Revelation 7:4
6. Matthew 6:24
7. 1 Timothy 2:4
8. Galatians 5:22-23
9. Revelation 19:14
10. Philippians 1:6
11. Revelation 19:11-12
12. Mark 13:32
13. 2 Corinthians 10:5
14. Mark 16:17
15. Romans 8:20-21
16. Matthew 7:21

CHAPTER 13

THE HEAVEN CONSPIRACY

*"But as for you, brethren, do not
grow weary in doing good."*

—2 THESSALONIANS 3:13

Ｔhe Heaven Conspiracy is a real, diabolical plan conceived by the devil. I received two visions that helped me to see the conspiracy so clearly.

In the first vision, I was in prayer and worship with some friends when I saw the front of the room turn into a playground. Suddenly, I was in Heaven.

In this vision, I was playing with my eldest grandbaby, Jerusalem. There were many families playing with their children.[1] Jesus was also there pushing the swings of children whose parents were not there. Everyone was laughing and enjoying the time together. The playground seemed state of the art. The ground was a bouncy pillow material so no child could get hurt. It was remarkable— as if the clouds themselves had left the sky to come and create a safety net. The play equipment was made of sturdy, living glass trees that offered themselves for climbing, swinging, and sliding. The swings had a special harness so the children could go so high as to actually swing over the top of the branch! And the slides were remarkable! They were tree vines that came together to create a huge, fast slide. Every ride on them was filled with big thrills and gleeful encounters.

I so enjoyed playing with Jerusalem. Eventually, we collapsed, exhausted in the rest area near the playground. She curled up beside me on a chaise lounge big enough for us both. The amazing chair seemed to have clouds for its cushions as well, and it conformed to us, providing perfect rest for our bodies. While we sat there, Jerusalem talked about many things that were in her heart. Jerusalem is a beautiful child who has a "justice chip" inside of her. She wants things to be right and fair, but in her lack of wisdom her ways, like mine, are not always the Lord's ways.

Her questions always began with "why," to which I had very few answers. She shared things about her goals and her wishes to be like me. I gently guided her back to the reality that everyone wants to be like Jesus and encouraged her to set Him as her goal. We watched the clouds and tried to spy animal representations in them as the wind moved them past. We watched the trees blow in the wind as if dancing and tried to name a tune to go with their dance. With each passing moment, our hearts grew closer. There was safety in being in the "playground" that Jesus created for us. There was not only safety, but the Lord provided spiritual growth too. You see, the playground was where God taught children about His nature.

Suddenly, there was a loud boom. We both sat up. It was coming from an area far away from the playground. Others around us quickly got up and went to see what it was. Jerusalem wanted to go too. Thinking back, I should not have gone. I should have stopped her from going! I should have followed the Lord's lead and stayed safely at the playground, but I acted without thinking or consulting Jesus.

As we approached the area where the sound had originated, I saw people jumping over a small brick wall. The wall went as far as my eyes could see both to the left and the right. I could have climbed over it, but Jerusalem, being smaller, would have a hard time getting across. The wall was purposefully made that way to protect the young ones. Unfortunately, I was too dull to realize that we were in great danger.

Jerusalem heard many children on the other side. They knew her name. They called out to her to come play with them. She questioned why the wall had been placed here and why those children were not allowed to come over.

I tried to explain that to play in *this* playground you have to believe in the Lord Jesus Christ as your personal Savior. I am not sure my quick answer was enough for her young curiosity as she was a babe in Christ. She then tried to explain what I had told her, but because she did not have a living understanding of this concept, it confused her. It was this confusion that caused her to begin to tune me out. The growing group of children enticed her to come to their side. I wish I had noticed the spirit of seduction that was being used against Jerusalem. Seduction is such that it lures you to look at something you think you want, and then it has you![2]

Jerusalem loves people, and of course she would want to go over to where there were so many new friends. They assured her that they do believe in Jesus. I knew that this type of belief is the same as when the demons say that they believe in Jesus, but somehow my words were spilling out in the wrong emotion, which only confused Jerusalem more.[3] They used it to convince her that I didn't care about them. To her, it was as if I was being mean to them. I explained that believing means that you must obey Jesus.[4] She tried to understand how believing means obeying, but she was confused. Suddenly, her justice chip was being used against me, and her reactions moved into mere human compassion for the other children. Human compassion is a good thing unless the enemy is using it.

Before I could grab her, she somehow climbed over the wall. Instantly, the wall began growing taller. She would not be able to return easily, if at all. As I jumped to get on top of the wall, I could see that a moat was built on that side, which made the wall way too tall. It became impossible for her to climb back over alone. I began to jump down, but instantly the Holy Spirit warned me that if I did, there would be no way for me to come back to this side. I understood immediately that if I went to that side, I would no longer be able to help anyone, myself included.

I am a vessel who has seen God in many visions. I do not have the luxury of responding immaturely like I had when I was a new Christian. I have been given much, and scripture teaches, "To whom much is given, much is required."[5] Let me try to explain what the Holy Spirit shared in with this vision. If I jumped over to that side, I would be emptying my light and filling myself with darkness. The Bible says it this way: "If the light that is in you is darkness, how dark then is the darkness inside of you."[6]

So I used my stern voice to call Jerusalem back. At that, she stopped and began to return. I am sure she could hear the panic in my voice. I demanded that she jump up and try to get my hand. Before she could try, many others joined the children standing around and they all began telling her I was mean. They told her that I was too strict and didn't want her to have fun. They sneered at her about how I even treat her like a baby. Suddenly I could see there were two groups—demons dressed like children and the lost children who had jumped over the wall.[7]

I looked and could find no one able to convince the children who had gone over the wall to not go further. Although I did not personally know all the children, I knew I could not abandon them.[8] These babes in Christ needed help. I was highly upset about all the children who were safe just seconds ago and now were in such danger.[9]

I knew that I was there to see something important. I was in the playground with Jerusalem learning how to disciple others.[10]

I learned that it requires listening, caring, having fun together, and doing the same things together regardless of which person is better at them. Jerusalem was faster on the slides than me! I had no idea where the other children's disciplers were.[11] I asked all the little ones to come over so I could help them come back to the good playground.

They all seemed to have that "justice chip" directing them and wanted nothing to do with me calling one place good and another bad. The demons told them how I was old-fashioned and didn't care about advancement.

Demons dressed like children took not only Jerusalem's hands but the others as well.[12] They were luring those with the justice chip to come away from the wall.

In my panic I yelled at Jerusalem to come back immediately or else. This was definitely the wrong move. Surrounded by so much darkness, I watched her eyes turn dark and her heart grow cold toward me. I could also see the eyes of the demons flash and the wicked smiles on their faces. They continued to walk her and the others farther away to a dangerous discipleship playground. This one was designed to hurt someone at every turn, but because Jerusalem was young, she could not see that.

The ground was covered in broken glass that quickly tore up the bottom of her shoes and began slicing her feet. They were moving her quickly, and she fell down. As they dragged her across the glass it ripped her knees and hands. As she cried, they hurled insults at her, but somehow she did not think about coming back.

Instead, she kept up the insanity of trying to fit in with them, as did the others who were there.

They put her on a slide. The slide was burning hot metal. If she sat on it, she would be burned. I watched as she slid down, and her clothes caught on fire. As she screamed in agony, they laughed and taunted her about what a big baby she was. I could see them enticing her to try the illicit drugs that they were using. She did, and although it dulled her pain, it allowed them to take her farther away from the wall.

I am sure that my voice was filled with the desperation that I felt inside. As I called her, the demons sang songs to drown out my voice. I grew deathly nauseous. My heart was breaking, my body shook with deep wrenching sobs, and I soon lost my voice from calling out for her.

Jerusalem and the others were being bombarded with lies and propaganda that would keep them away.[13] At the same time, the wall continued to grow taller and narrowed to the point that it was as if I was now standing on a tight rope. There was a fight in the winds like one wind was trying to keep me on the side of Jesus while the other was trying to push me off of the wall and into the darkness.

I no longer had a voice for yelling or tears for crying. I had spent everything in the desperation of watching my grandbaby sink further into deception. Still I sent the silent wind out of my lungs, *"Jesus, help me!"*

Suddenly, in the midst my desperation, I felt strong hands grab the calves of my legs. As I looked down, I saw an intercessor sitting on top on a long string of intercessors securing me to the wall.[14] They were connected to one another and were unmovable. They were praying for Jerusalem and for me. I told them that there were *many* other children who were there as well. I shared how we must try to bring them *all* back. Because they were intercessors, they understood my silent words.[15]

I could hear their prayers as they called for the Holy Spirit to come! They also prayed for all the children to hear what the Spirit was saying to the Church.[16] They kept asking Jesus to come. Instantly, He was on the wall holding my hand. My voice was once again strong and louder than any attempt of the demons to silence it. This time I knew that I was using His strength. The last thing to leave a person before they die is their hearing, and so I knew Jerusalem could still hear me with the help of Jesus.

I cried out again and again, *"O Jerusalem, Jerusalem, how I love you! Come back! Come to the wall! Come now! Jerusalem, follow the sound of my voice! I want you. I need you. Come quickly!"*

As I was saying this over and over, I heard the Lord call out to the others, *"O Jerusalem, Jerusalem, how I have longed to gather you!"[17] Jerusalem, how I love you! Come quickly! Come quickly!"*

The vision ended, and I was shaken! It was noticeable to my friends that something had happened to me. I frantically told them the vision as I cried. They assured me that my grandbaby was home with my daughter, but I could not rest until I could see her for myself and see that she was OK.

Today, I have built a strong relationship with Jerusalem and her siblings. I take their growth in God very seriously.[18] I disciple them while times are easy so that they will know how to stay close to Jesus when times are hard. And it's not just for them, but for the others around them because this generation seems to have that justice chip.

In the second vision that the Lord used to reveal the Heaven Conspiracy to me, I was standing on a mountain with other gospel workers. The mountain was huge—at least 50 miles high and 100 miles around. People were brought in the Spirit to this mountain before they would die. They came because they had not received the Lord as Savior in their lifetime. Most of the people did not realize that their time was short, but for the few who did, they didn't care. Some of the people truly believed that they were on the mount because they chose to be. The truth was that the Lord had brought them for another chance to see Him for who He is. There were many who could not see how satan had stopped them from recognizing Jesus. Others were of religions that hated Jesus or discounted Him altogether.

Everyone on the mountain was a sinner.[19] The difference was that the workers had repented of their sins. The Lord will forgive and had forgiven sins such as abortion, lying, stealing, cheating, pornography, and the list goes on and on. All of these sins, along with sexual immorality, witchcraft, jealousy, selfish ambition, and envy were punishable with eternal damnation.[20] Sliding off the mountain was the reward these sins had earned each person who rejected Jesus.

In this vision, I had some supernatural qualities.[21] I could see perfectly, was extremely strong, and was unable to be moved by the forces of evil around me because I sat by God. I wore green camou-flage from my helmet to my clothes and army boots. Additionally, I wore green makeup on my exposed skin. I understood that *green* is the color of life. I also wore a safety harness that was connected to a massive helicopter. The helicopter was a rescue machine sent on behalf of Heaven. There were many workers dropping from the aircraft. Each was tied to a cord that could quickly bring them to safety. There were also many angels dropping cords that had hooks on the end. All together we were far too few to accomplish the colossal job before us.[22]

I personally knew two of the workers, both evangelists, who were dressed similarly to me. One was shouting, *"Do not grow weary doing this good work!"*[23] The other was bent over, and I watched the muscles on his calves shake from exhaustion. I, too, was exhausted, but the task was of the utmost importance. When we were fin-ished, the mountain would be empty, one way or another.

The mountain was very slippery, and the boots I wore pro-vided my feet the security I needed to not slide. I was near the bottom of the mountain looking up toward the peak. Hell opened wide below us at the bottom edge of the mountain. I stood where I did because I had knowledge of hell. Most of the evangelists stood at the bottom because they are bold enough to tell the whole truth about eternity.

The mountain was so slippery because it was covered from top to bottom with counterfeit oil. It was oil but a false kind with no benefits. It was not like the oil that we receive in spending time with God and learning His ways.[24] Some people had covered their whole selves in this oil so that they could slide past us, and even if we could connect with them it was like trying to catch a slippery fish. Multitudes of people were sliding down the mountain and into hell. It was devastating. With each person who passed me on his or her way to eternal torture, my spirit cried out! It was all so reckless and unnecessary.

My job was to quickly preach the gospel of Jesus one last time. The pressure of that knowledge was unthinkable. However, I had no time to think. Later I could cry all I wanted. At that moment I had to stay focused because time was coming to an end.

The years of practice I'd had before were the Lord's training for this crucial time. If the people agreed to follow Jesus, I would use one of the hooked cables to attach the person to the safety line. Then an angel was waiting to hoist them to safety. The crisis I faced was that for every person I could stop and convince that Jesus was the only way, 250 people slid past.

This dire situation was the same for all of the workers. The sheer numbers of people who were gleefully going to hell devastated everyone.

There were some people sliding down who worshiped the devil. They tried to take as many other people as possible with them to hell. There were people who would not listen no matter what. They had so much pride and hatred in their hearts toward the gospel. Not only did they not want to hear the saving gospel, but they kept the young ones away from us by intentionally sliding them away from us. It was horrible!

I looked down to see a person barely holding on to the edge of the cliff. I reached down with the hook and even though he did not want to go to hell, he *refused* to let Jesus be Lord of his life. I watched that person fall into hell screaming.

The mountain seemed pleasant to the natural eye. The heat from hell didn't touch the people. It was a sunny day, and everything looked just fine. Even though the workers of the harvest were yelling at people, those sliding down weren't panicked or desperate, and most didn't see the danger looming. They had no idea of the hour they were living in and refused to listen to the truths from the gospel workers.

My whole body wrenched from the pain of watching so many go to hell. I heard the evangelists yell out again, *"Do not grow weary in this good work that you do!"* It strengthened me to try again.[25]

Yes, there is a conspiracy about Heaven. Unfortunately, many are being deceived into it.[26] Satan has come to steal, kill, and destroy! He understands that God has God-sized boundaries. God cannot lie or be a respecter of persons. If God said it, then He has to do it.[27] The law is the law, and all of mankind has sinned, meaning all of mankind is headed to hell.[28] It is that simple.

Satan's evilness works to deceive the multitudes in hope that when they realize his ploy, it will be too late. He basically uses two approaches—deny that Heaven exists or present Heaven as a place that everyone goes when they die. There are many half-truths and complete lies that he uses in this conspiracy. His plan is to lull all of mankind into a false comfort and ultimately take them to hell.

Our *only* hope is in Jesus Christ, the only way to the Father in Heaven.[29]

Satan will do anything within his power to stop people from encountering Jesus so that they will never enter Heaven. He works hard at making Heaven, or God for that matter, a figment of the imagination. He whispers, *"If there was a Heaven, and if God could see, then He would not let people starve, die, be human trafficked, or suffer terrible things."* And many fall for his distortion of the truth.

Satan loves to use grief-filled times such as the loss of a treasure, job, relationship, or the death of a loved one to attack a person's trust in God. In those difficult times, he whispers that if there was a Heaven with a wonderful God, this could have never happened.[30]

Satan twists the truths of science.[31] He uses lies such as evolution, aliens, time travel, reincarnation, and carbon dating to attack the foundational truth that in the beginning God created the Heavens and the earth.

Satan has worked hard over the years deceiving mankind.[32] He tries to cast doubt over the Bible, which gives many examples of what Heaven is like. He has worked to create confusion on simple issues such as what is a male and a female or the truth that the child growing inside of a woman is really a baby. He has deceived people, leading them into deep sexual immorality and destroying the gifts of sex, marriage, and children. He has misled people, convincing them to leave one another in hard times by convincing them that they shouldn't suffer just because the other person was suffering.[33]

Today the family is a mess! Husbands and wives cheat on each other, leaving broken hearts and confusion about God. Mothers and fathers abort, abandon, steal from, control, and reject their children, leaving broken hearts and confusion about God. Children neglect their siblings, steal for and from their parents, and abandon the responsibilities of the family unit, leaving broken hearts and confusion about God.[34] Satan hates families!

Satan has created *many* false religions with countless people joining them. He rejoices at theism and has created his own false religions where he is worshiped. He has religions where the sun, a cow, a statue, and even yourself can be God.[35] All in an effort to cause us to forget that God is the maker of Heaven, earth, and mankind.[36] Each false religion is designed to deny Heaven and God so that people go to hell.

There are faiths that do not believe in the deity of Jesus, the inerrancy of the Bible, the baptism of the Holy Spirit, or hell as a literal place, and yet satan has still convinced them that they are Christian.[37]

Even if one *does* still believe there might be a Heaven, the devil has convinced multitudes not to worry because all religions and their ultimate paths eventually lead to Heaven and God.[38]

Inside of the Church, satan has also been hard at work. If a person believes in Heaven, satan works to twist the truth. He tells one group of people that Jesus is holy, and they could never measure up. To another group, he assures them "once saved, always saved" so it doesn't matter how they live. He persuades them that because God loves them so much and is so good, God would look the other way when it comes to their sin and do anything and everything to let them enter Heaven. Satan goes so far as to help individuals create their own list of rules that allow them to live how they please and to follow their own wicked desires.[39] In this, satan is lying and trying to convince them that sin is relative and God gives grace upon grace with no accountability on Judgment Day. Satan's lies include things like purgatory where a person can work off their sin. Of course, satan lets people in the Church believe that Jesus is the Savior, but blinds them to the necessity of having Jesus as *the Lord* of their lives.

Workers in intercession, discipleship, evangelism, and intimacy should be able to see the conspiracy clearly. These workers will be a lifeline, a last line of defense in exposing the Heaven Conspiracy.

We must pray for eyes to see the conspiracies and the dark deception that is happening around us! The Bible teaches that we must walk out our salvation with fear and trembling.[40] Our salvation is a treasure of great importance, and we do not want to lose it by being lazy, haphazard, or worse yet, willfully sinning.

We must understand what is necessary to comply with this teaching. For those who do not know Jesus as your personal Savior, this is of the utmost importance. You must repent and become a child of God before it is too late!

For those who are truly saved, you must take sin seriously and repent so that you are able to search for the ways of God.[41] Finally, every Christian should realize the importance of salvation and help others know Jesus while there is still time![42]

Repentance has four parts, and if we leave out a part then it is not true repentance. Without true repentance we cannot find mercy.[43]

First, you must agree with God that sin is sin. He decides what is sinful, and we need to align ourselves to His definition without exception.

Second, you must have godly sorrow over sin. This is much more than being sorry. If we are only sorry, we will commit the same sin over and over. Godly sorrow will cause you to stop sinning.

Third, you must confess your sin one to another.[44] This will help you become accountable and place a person in your life who will help you fight sin. This is not only a command from God but is proven to bring the right results.

Last, you need put something in place in your life to help you not fall the same way again. You must think of and implement a plan to stay out of sin. Your accountability person can help you along with the Holy Spirit.

Once you have repented, you need to pray and connect your heart and life to Jesus. I do not usually ask people to follow a specific prayer, but because we are not face to face, let me share with you a working example:

- Prepare to talk to God—go somewhere you are comfortable.
- Address God—make it personal, call Him by a name you honor.
- Tell Him what you believe about Him.

- Tell Him what you know—tell Him the truths that you know about Him.

- Tell him what sin you have done—admit your guilt.

- Tell Him the consequence—tell Him that you are headed to hell.

- Ask Him to forgive you—ask and wait for His answer.

- Thank Him—take your time.

- Ask for His help—don't leave until He tells you to go.

Although I want you to figure out what is right for you, I would suggest you find a Christian and do this together, out loud, so that your physical body and the atmosphere can hear you. Go to a quiet place where you will not be rushed and where you can close your eyes and picture Jesus.

With your spirit quiet, try to notice where Jesus is and what He is doing.

Begin with addressing Him as Your Honor, Almighty Father, Savior, or sweet Jesus. Choose something that lets your heart know to whom you are talking.

Let your heart speak words of what you believe, such as: *Lord, You have been so kind and patient with me all these years. You are the Creator of the world, and You are the only way to Heaven.*

Continue with what you know, such as: *Lord, I need Your help because I am desperate, sick of my life. I need You so that I can stop doing all the bad things.*[45]

Confess your sin, such as: *Jesus, I am a sinner. We both know that I lie, cheat, and steal. Help me confess everything so that I can be sure You see my desperate needs.*[46]

Share with Jesus how you know you deserve hell. Think on that for a time. Let the desperation of your situation sink in.

Humbly ask Him for His help. Ask Him if He would die for you and go to hell so that you won't. Wait for His answer.

Thank Jesus out loud from your heart.

Ask Jesus what ideas He can think of that will stop you from sinning that way again.

Then ask Jesus to be your closest and best friend. Ask Him for help to be water baptized and baptized in the Holy Spirit. Talk with Him daily and read the Bible. Worship God with music and with your giving.

With His help, He will keep us from evil and clearly expose every conspiracy designed to trap us. He will bring us to Heaven to be with Him forever. Until then, with this knowledge, we can connect others to Him.

NOTES

1. Psalm 37:18
2. 2 Corinthians 2:11
3. James 2:19

4. John 8:31
5. Luke 12:48
6. Matthew 6:23
7. Matthew 7:15
8. Philippians 2:4
9. John 10:10
10. Romans 10:14-15
11. John 10:12
12. Ephesians 6:11
13. John 8:44
14. 1 Timothy 2:8
15. Matthew 18:19-20, Matthew 21:22
16. Revelation 2:11, Revelation 2:29
17. Matthew 23:37, Luke 13:34
18. Proverbs 22:6
19. Romans 3:23
20. Galatians 5:20-21
21. 2 Timothy 3:17
22. Matthew 9:37, Luke 10:2
23. Galatians 6:9
24. Matthew 25:1-13
25. Galatians 6:9
26. John 10:10
27. Numbers 23:19
28. Romans 3:23
29. John 3:16, John 14:6
30. Ezekiel 33:11, 2 Peter 3:9
31. 1 Timothy 6:20

32. John 8:44, 2 Corinthians 11:14, 2 Thessalonians 2:9-10

33. Jeremiah 17:9

34. 2 Timothy 3:2

35. Habakkuk 2:18

36. Psalm 50:22

37. Acts 8:18-19, 2 Timothy 3:5

38. John 14:6

39. Matthew 16:24

40. Philippians 2:12

41. Acts 3:19

42. James 4:8

43. Proverbs 28:13

44. James 5:16

45. Matthew 3:8

46. 1 John 1:9

CHAPTER 14

◆◆◆

THE PARADE

"This is the day the Lord has made; we will rejoice and be glad in it."

—PSALM 118:24

I would like to share with you one more heavenly vision that will help all of us with our own personal bridal walk like I shared about in the first chapter.

When I arrived in Heaven in this vision, I heard loud cheers. I was at a parade and it was so exciting! Suddenly, people standing around me began hugging me. They were so glad that I was there. I heard them say to others, *"She has never seen the parade."*

Because everyone in Heaven is incredibly nice, the crowd began parting so that I could reach the front. As I moved closer toward the street to see the parade, I looked down and saw the rocks moving me as if I was on a conveyor belt.

I was in such awe! Everyone was welcoming me, and there was a celebratory atmosphere.[1] The parade was for a day that the Lord had made.[2] It was a celebration of a particular day that was lived on earth before I was born. Because I do not specifically remember the exact date, let's say the parade was in honor of May 1, 1964.

One of the first things that I noticed were the spectacularly shiny, spinning drops, much like confetti, falling from the sky. They were amazing—like a liquid love. When they hit a person like a drop of rainwater, they would quickly be absorbed, causing great delight. The droplets that hit the ground would scurry over to the closest person and be absorbed through their feet. I watched the drops and was mesmerized by the sight. A person on my right hugged me and encouraged me to watch the parade itself. I was so glad that they were helping me, or I would only be able to tell of the wondrous droplets. For me, it was like when I was a child going to see the three-ring circus; there was just no way take it all in.[3]

On my left was a man who was filled with regret. I found this very strange because everyone else around me was filled with joy. I have never felt regret in Heaven before. It was as if this regret was allowed somehow.

In the parade, there were multitudes of people marching. The knowledge was granted to me regarding why those people were being highlighted in the parade.[4] They were the ones who had been alive on May 1, 1964 and they had served the Lord in some way. He was honoring what they had done for Him, either large or small, with this extravagant parade.[5]

In the parade, there was a shy, tall man walking. I could tell that he was the quiet type. Many people were shouting out for him and clapping. On that particular day in history, this man had stopped to help someone change a tire. It was his love for Jesus that had compelled him to help. At the parade, the Lord honored this man and shared with everyone what he had done out of the goodness of his life in Christ.

Also part of the procession was a short, round woman who had a very different personality. She was exceptionally lively, quite chatty, and extremely upbeat. She was waving at those of us who were lining the street. Many were also shouting and clapping for her. She had served a family who had just had a new baby by baking and delivering a fancy cake. She had spent many hours making this cake extra special. The family had miscarried their last baby, and she wanted to help make this celebration exceptional. Although she had no idea her action would be celebrated this way when she baked the cake, her service delighted Jesus.

The parade was filled with people who had done amazing things for Jesus, but there was another man who really stood out to me.[6] He had died on that day because he would not deny Jesus.[7] The crowd went wild in their clapping and shouting for him. This man walked with tears running down his face. He was a tender man who wore his heart on his sleeve. He was very big and strong. He had not used his physical strength against the Lord's enemies but had shared the gospel so that they might be saved.[8] Everyone knew that this man had been given this unique opportunity because the Lord already knew the outcome.

Each of these highlighted ones had done things that day, from something as small as giving a cup of cold water to laying down one's life.[9] And each was emphasized and highlighted as a monumental action. It was the best celebration ever!

However, the parade did not single one person out, but rather put on display what people had done collectively for the love of Jesus. May 1, 1964 was incredibly remarkable because normal, common people showed their love in stunning ways. The parade allowed us to know why that day was so special to God![10]

As I was again focused on the droplets that were running over to me and filling me up, I could do nothing but squeal in delight. The person behind me hugged me and pointed for me to try to pay attention to what was happening in the parade—my very purpose for being there.

As I looked, I saw a magnificent horse. There was some distance between the people and him, which only made him more impressive. He was absolutely stunning and taller than any horse I had ever seen. On this day, he was extra alert and proud. He had so much personality! Through the gift of knowledge, I could understand him perfectly. He was strutting his stuff all decked out in brilliant materials and skipping while performing a complicated dance. His mane was shimmering from all the droplets that had fallen on him. Flowing down his side was a material that touched the ground and caused a ripple effect of mini shock-waves to go out from him. Whenever they touched anything in the mind, will, emotions, or physical realms, it was healed.

I looked closely at the hem of the rider's cloak, which was covered in leaves. It was not an embroidery or material leaf pattern, but they were real leaves as if someone had just picked them off of a tree and placed them on the hem. They were not sewn onto the cloak. Instead, they had made the choice to hug the hem of the garment. These leaves bordered the entire cloak. Incredibly, they too sent out shock waves of healing to the left, right, and behind. I thought that the droplets were amazing, yet the ripples of healing were a million times more amazing. Every remarkable thing I saw in Heaven could easily consume all my focus!

As I was transfixed watching the effects of the wondrous things in Heaven, the regretful man on my left suddenly joined in the parade. I felt his regret turn to joy. You see, the man had lived that day, May 1, but he had done nothing for God that would allow him to march in the parade. However, he had been alive, and the Lord had been working mightily in him so that eventually the man had come to love and serve Jesus.[11] Because of this, he was able to join the parade once the horse passed. His walking in the parade declared God's mighty ability to win a heart and complete the good work that He had begun![12] The man walked very proudly, as did the others who were joining in behind the horse.

The people standing around me asked me what I thought of the Lord in His splendor. I explained that I had not seen the Lord. They were all surprised that I had not noticed the man, *the Lord*, riding atop of His horse. I was upset that I had missed Jesus!

As they shared down the line that I had not seen Jesus, once again a path opened so that the rocks could move me up the parade route. My hope was to quickly get in front of the horse again so that I could see Jesus' face.

Now I knew the horse was the Lord's, and I understood why he was so proud—He carried Jesus! In Heaven, people, angels, animals, and other living things are not jealous of each other because everything was created for a specific purpose. When each did what they were created for, they brought joy to the Lord. The horse knew that he was the Lord's and anything less than being exuberant would have been false.

As I moved forward, I enjoyed watching the horse from the back perform his dance. Seeing how excited he was to be the Lord's personal horse made me excited that I am Laurie, His child.

When I neared the Lord and His horse, my attention was drawn to the ground where I noticed huge amounts of healing ripples and droplets being sent for me. Then I looked up where I could see that the cloak covering the horse was actually resting on the shoulders of the Man who rode it. And, to my surprise, I saw that the drops of liquid love raining down on us were coming from Jesus. He was the source of all of the liquid love, and He was sending it up into the atmosphere so it was coming down like confetti everywhere.

Then I noticed something that caused me to instantly stop, drop, and release a sound of extreme, overwhelming gratitude like I have never heard or uttered before.

I saw the Lord's crown perched on His head as He rode. It was shocking and fulfilling at the same time. His crown was a thick glass crown of thorns. It shone with the most brilliant light!

Only this mighty King could ever wear the crown of thorns![13] I knew—the crown of thorns was not only at the Cross, and it is not something of which He was ashamed. He wore it as a symbol of the reason why every single day is a gift. His crown showed the great love He has for the Father and for us. It exemplified His complete obedience. Of course, Jesus would wear a symbol of submission to His Father and an example for His people.

I could not contain my thankfulness and my awe. I fell on the rocks and sobbed. As I sobbed, my heart released a sound. I was still making that sound when I returned to the earth. The memory of this sound makes me want to empty my ways and desire His.

There will be many parades of days that I have lived throughout my lifetime—too many that I will not be able to walk before the Lord's great horse. But because of what Jesus did on the Cross for me and for mankind, I now have knowledge that opened my heart to everlasting gratitude and love for Him and His selfless act. Because of Him, thankfully, each of those days I will be able to walk behind it. Like the man on my left, I feel regret for not having lived for the Lord. I cannot go back, but I can live purposefully each day forward.[14]

My purpose in sharing this vision is that our greatest prayer and lifelong goal will be to do small and great acts of love for Jesus. Remember that the Lord will celebrate every day in a parade. And best of all, those acts that we do will be highlighted and become a sweet offering to the Lord.[15]

Hopefully, you now yearn for Heaven with great anticipation! May this book fill you with longings for adventures, dances, and surprises with Jesus because He can make them all a reality. Take your wishes for benefitting others on your bridal march, and remember that each caring act will place you in a parade celebrating that very day.

Invite everyone—your family, friends, co-workers, and acquaintances—to desire the King and the Kingdom of Heaven as their home.

May you also feel challenged to live like you belong in Heaven and make every moment count, because they do!

NOTES

1. Romans 5:1-3
2. Psalm 118:24
3. Matthew 18:3
4. Matthew 5:16
5. Revelations 22:12, Colossians 3:23-24, Galatians 6:9, 1 Corinthians 2:9, Romans 2:6
6. Acts 6:15
7. Revelation 6:9
8. Mark 16:15
9. Matthew 10:42
10. Psalm 118:24
11. Philippians 1:6
12. Philippians 1:6
13. John 19:2
14. 1 Corinthians 15:54
15. 1 Corinthians 13:13

About Laurie A. Ditto

Laurie A. Ditto travels around the world sharing her testimonies of Heaven and hell to reach people for Jesus. As director of My Father's Reputation, she trains people in the prophetic to hear Jesus for others. Laurie and Mike have been married for 38 years. They have two daughters and twelve grandchildren.

Other Books by Laurie A. Ditto

Go. Tell Others about Me

The Hell Conspiracy